Backroad Bicycling in the Hudson Valley and Catskills

Backroad Bicycling in the Hudson Valley and Catskills

PETER KICK &
DORI O'CONNELL

THE COUNTRYMAN PRESS
WOODSTOCK, VERMONT

For Claude and Marie Post, Dori's Mom and Dad

An Invitation to the Reader
Although it is unlikely that the roads you cycle on these tours will change much
with time, some road signs, landmarks, and other terms may. If you find that
changes have occurred on these routes, please let us know so we may correct
them in future editions. Address all correspondence to:

Editor
Bicycling Guides
The Countryman Press
P.O. Box 748
Woodstock, VT 05091

Copyright © 2006 by Peter Kick and Dori O'Connell
First Edition

ISBN-10: 0-88150-578-1
ISBN-13: 978-0-88150-578-8

Published by The Countryman Press, PO Box 748, Woodstock, VT 05091
Distributed by W. W. Norton & Company, Inc., 500 Fifth Avenue, New York,
NY 10110

Text and cover design by Bodenweber Design
Composition by Maggie Dana
Cover photograph by Dennis Coello
Maps by Tony Moore/Moore Creative Designs © The Countryman Press
Interior photographs by the authors

Printed in the United States of America

10 9 8 7 6 5 4 3 2 1

ACKNOWLEDGMENTS We'd like to thank everyone who has helped us along the way, including the folks whose names we never learned. Among the known, we'd like to thank Mike Anelli, owner of Village Bicycles in Millerton, for The Miller's Tale tour. We'd like to thank Terry Paddock of the Accord Bicycle Service for route advice, and for offering his shop lot as a parking place for Terry's Shop Ride. We'd like to thank Gil Hales and Mike Harkavy for the Saugerties loops—together (and facing substantial odds) they brought Saugerties kicking and screaming into the greenway era. We'd like to thank Billy Denter of the Overlook Bike Shop in Woodstock for his enthusiasm and encouragement, and for telling us a thing or two about bikes. Thanks also go to our longtime friend Joe Clark, bike ranger at Mohonk, a great resource for biking in the preserve, and to riding partners Barry Knight and Rita Berman. Thanks go to Bill Kennedy at Kenco, the work and play outfitter, for his support and friendship. Finally, special thanks for his patience and support go to Kermit Hummel, Editor in Chief of The Countryman Press, and to Jennifer Thompson, Managing Editor.

BICYCLE TOURS AT A GLANCE

RIDE NUMBER/NAME	REGION	DISTANCE
1. De Zaagertjes: Saugerties	Catskills	14/18
2. Beyond the Great Vly: High Falls	Catskills	27.5
3. Zanzibar: The Great Eastern Cloves	Catskills	20.6
4. All Creation, Lad: North Lake Loop	Catskills	7.3
5. Huck and the Huckleberry: Tannersville	Catskills	12
6. Fire and Rain: The Schoharie Reservoir	Catskills	14.3
7. A Million Sides Tanned: Prattsville	Catskills	15
8. Flick's Fix: The Spruceton Valley	Catskills	10
9. YMCA: Frost Valley	Catskills	28
10. One More Notch: The Eastern Catskills	Catskills	42.6
11. Three Days of Peace and Music: Woodstock	Catskills	13.2
12. A Few Red Cents: Denning	Catskills	17/11.2
13. The Holy Grail: Peekamoose Clove to Vernooy Kill Falls	Catskills	35

DIFFICULTY	BIKE TYPE	NOTES
Easy/Moderate	Mtn, hybrid, road	River and mountain scenery; antiques shops
Strenuous	Mtn, hybrid, road	Waterfall, beaver meadows, forest and mountain scenery
Strenuous	Mtn, hybrid, road	Kaaterskill Falls is off route; a mountainous ride through two deep gorges
Easy	Mtn, hybrid	Beautiful backdrop of high hills, scenic views of Hudson Valley; camping, swimming, and hiking trails at North Lake Public Campground, kids O.K.
Moderate	Mtn, hybrid, road	Forested scenic ride through Catskill Mountain culture and Huckleberry Trail; kids o.k. on rail trail only
Moderate	Mtn, hybrid	Historic Gilboa Dam, fossilized giant tree ferns, wooded roads past reservoir
Strenuous	Mtn, hybrid, road	Scenic rolling hills, Pratt's Rocks—historic carvings in the mountainside
Easy	Mtn, hybrid, road	Alpine landscape of a high valley next to a trout stream
Strenuous	Mtn, hybrid, road	Scenic ride through upper-elevation wilderness next to trout streams
Strenuous	Mtn, hybrid, road	Hills and rivers through a historic mountain pass and the mountain towns of Tannersville, Phoenicia, and Woodstock
Strenuous	Mtn, hybrid, road	Historic village, Byrdcliffe Art Colony and Theater, scenic high peaks, a zen monastery
Easy/Moderate	Mtn, hybrid, road	Beautiful ride along a trout stream in the interior Catskills; high scenic return loop
Strenuous	Mtn, hybrid	The interior Catskill Forest Preserve of rivers and wild forest; Vernooy Kill Falls

DIFFICULTY	BIKE TYPE	NOTES
Easy	Mtn, hybrid, road	Amazing scenic views of the Catskill High Peaks, eagle nesting area; kids O.K. on areas closed to traffic
Easy	Mtn, hybrid	Ride along the Rondout Creek and D&H Towpath next to creek; kids O.K. on towpath only
Moderate	Mtn, hybrid, road	Old farm roads and scenic hilly lands, historic village of High Falls with stone canal locks
Strenuous	Mtn, hybrid, road	Scenic Shawangunks, northern Shawangunks ridge, historic Mohonk Mountain House and Mohonk Gateway Center
Easy	Mtn, hybrid	The carriage roads of the Shawangunks, Trapps rock climbing, Mohonk Gateway Center; kids o.k.
Moderate	Mtn, hybrid, road	The Wallkill Valley Rail Trail, New Paltz historic district
Moderate	Mtn, hybrid, road	Beautiful hills and flats through agricultural lands
Moderate	Mtn, hybrid	Gently rolling farm country with views of Catskill
Strenuous	Mtn, hybrid	Rambling farm roads and forest; Steepletop, the poet Edna St. Vincent Millay's home and workplace; Millay Poetry Trail
Strenuous	Mtn, hybrid	Large open spaces of fields and farms, views of the Taconic plateau
Strenuous	Mtn, hybrid	Forested area of southern Taconics; Bash Bish Falls (off route); Harlem Valley Rail Trail; camping, swimming, and hiking trails at Taconic State Park
Moderate	Mtn, hybrid	Beautiful back roads of the Copake Hills, Taconic State Park nearby (camping, swimming, hiking trails)

DIFFICULTY	BIKE TYPE	NOTES
Strenuous	Mtn, hybrid	Undiscovered, rugged backcountry ride; Bash Bish Falls (off route); Taconic State Park; Rudd Pond state campground (camping, swimming, hiking trails)
Easy	Mtn, hybrid, road	Perfect forested family ride on the paved Harlem Valley Rail Trail; Taconic State Park at the trailhead (camping, swimming, hiking trails); kids O.K.
Easy	Mtn, hybrid, road	The quaint village of Tivoli with sleepy back roads leading to farm country and dense woods; Clermont Mansion on the Hudson River
Moderate/Strenuous	Mtn, hybrid, road	Old Rhinebeck Aerodrome; back roads to farmsteads and quiet woods
Moderate	Mtn, hybrid, road	Hilly county roads and backcountry byways with extraordinary scenery; Harlem Valley Rail Trail access
Strenuous	Mtn, hybrid, road	Old farm and forest roads with wild charm past Thompson Pond, a national natural landmark with nesting golden eagles
Easy	Mtn, hybrid, road	Rich farmlands, views across the Hudson and into the Catskill Mountains, Rhinebeck's historic village and Poet's Walk Park
Moderate	Mtn, hybrid, road	Quiet, timeless back roads connecting little farms and hamlets
Moderate	Mtn, hybrid, road	A sweet ride through wooded hollows and dairy farms
Easy	Mtn	Eleanor Roosevelt's home, Val-Kill, connects to FDR's home, Springwood, through a large parcel of woods
Moderate	Mtn, hybrid, road	Rich woodlands, quiet back roads along old horse farms, and lovely homes; a visit to the Institute of Ecosystem Studies; village of Millbrook

DIFFICULTY	BIKE TYPE	NOTES
Strenuous	Mtn, hybrid, road	Ride on the oldest state road in the Colonies (Post Road), through pre-Revolutionary iron mine country and past lakes and woodlands
Moderate	Mtn, hybrid, road	A scenic ride along the extensive reservoir system and woodsy hinterlands around the town of Carmel

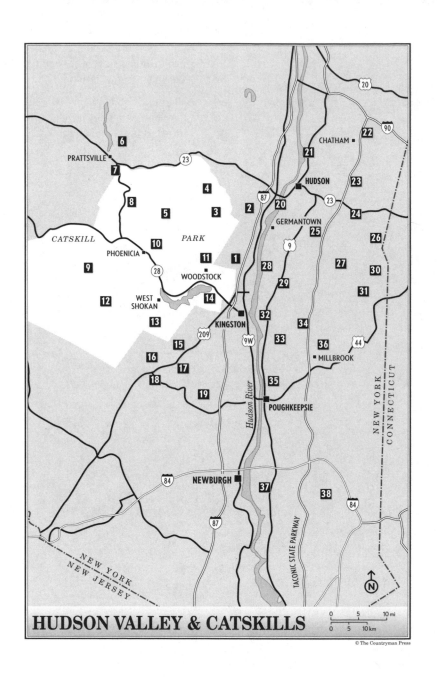

HUDSON VALLEY & CATSKILLS

© The Countryman Press

CONTENTS

INTRODUCTION The Hudson River Valley is a national treasure. In recognition of that fact, the national park service dedicated it as a national heritage area (HRVHA) in 1996. The designation encompasses the Valley itself, defined as the 10 counties along the Hudson's banks between Albany and Yonkers. Within that 150-mile stretch there are almost 4 million acres, 12 cities, 42 towns, 26 villages, and almost 3 million people. The thing that surprises many people is that only about 5 percent of the open space in the Valley is public, protected space. This book focuses on the most scenic open spaces in the Hudson Valley, and the least populated—the Mid-Hudson region.

Beginning in the Adirondacks' Lake Tear of the Clouds, the Hudson River flows 315 miles through eastern New York State to the Battery, draining an area of 13,000 miles. What makes the river so richly scenic is the fact that, geologically, the Hudson is a fjord—a narrow coastal inlet with steep sides created by glacial action. It is one of only two places where the great Appalachian Chain is breached by flowing water (in the Highlands region). Significant mountain ranges like the Catskills, Shawangunks, and Taconics rise near to its banks, and any cyclist who completes the tours in this book will become acquainted with all of them.

The Hudson Valley is so interesting because the river provided the first major commercial and settlement artery into the New Frontier, the place that would ultimately become America, as we know it. Inhabited peacefully for thousands of years by indigenous peoples of the Paleo and Woodland periods, it was occupied by the Dutch, seized by British, and retaken by the Continental Army under George Washington. Unsettled and violent as it was, the events of the Revolutionary War left the rich legacy of places and things that visitors to the

area see today: an heirloom landscape of uncommon variety and signifi-
cance. The Hudson Valley was named a National Heritage Area in
recognition of these cultural, historic, and scenic assets, all of which
combine to form an important part of our national identity. That identity has a lot to do with the things a cyclist will see in the Hudson
Valley, as nearly every town reflects some aspect of this deeply tex-
tured history.

But, what about the terrain? This bike book is defined by the Hudson
Valley and its subregion, the Catskill Mountains. It includes the
smaller mountain ranges of the Shawangunks in the Mid-Hudson
Valley, and the Taconics that lay along the western boundary of New
York State. In very general terms, the three counties on the east side
of the Hudson River—Putnam in the south, Dutchess in the middle,
and Columbia to the north—make for easier rides than the western
mountainous areas of the Catskills and the Shawangunks (the *Gunks*).
Each of these counties on the east side of the river is heavily agricultural, now as they were long ago, and accordingly they are characterized by rich, fertile lowlands split by slow meandering rivers. These
rivers were formed in the early earth-building Taconic Orogeny when
Himalayan-sized mountains covered the region, and much later they
were shaped by glaciers into low, rolling hills. Although some of these
hills may be very steep in places, they are by nature not long and difficult, and vertical rise tends to be distributed over the length of the tour,
rather than concentrated into isolated, extended climbs. The exception
to this is the two Taconic area tours that climb over the Taconic plateau
into Massachusetts (Rides 24 and 26). Both rides involve the steep
climb through Bash Bish Gorge before relaxing on the upper west side
of the mountain range and tapering into long glides to the south and
north, respectively.

In the Catskills, cyclists will find more challenging hills, and rides
that take place at higher elevations, some of which are in wilderness
areas that require more careful planning and preparation. Many of
these tours begin with a long ascent, rising out of the Valley into areas
that were kept pristine as the result of large land patents, and later
preserved by an act of Congress as today's forest preserve. Not only are
these areas more remote, where the cyclist will find fewer services (and

in some cases none) and fewer residences for long distances, they are also more exposed in terms of wind and climactic change, and up to 10 degrees cooler on average than the Valley itself. The possibility for exposure certainly exists, and cyclists, especially when both perspiring as well as expending large quantities of energy, can put themselves at risk by lack of preparedness. Be certain (as with every tour) to carry enough food and water, to dress in layers and carry raingear, and to review the logistics of every trip carefully before setting out. Don't hesitate to abandon the itinerary and turn around or shortcut back—you can always return another day.

Because the Mid-Hudson Valley is the place where we live, and where we have done the greatest share of our recreational riding, it has been the area of interest and focus for this book. Not only are there many more possibilities for rides in the described areas, there are extensive blocks of territory both north and south that could fill volumes. And so we have not written this book under the pretense that what lies within its pages is the best the region has to offer, and if any such boasts exist either here, or in other places, they are not our own. What we have sought to bring forth is a representative offering of our own favorite places within the realm where we live and ride—the unforgettable storied places, blue hills, furrowed fields, and clear-running streams of the Hudson River Valley and the Catskills. From your own experiences, you can build new and exciting routes beyond these. We hope you enjoy them as much as we have, and will return often.

ROUTE FINDING It's never a question of finding enough material for the creation of a cycling book. Instead, it's an exercise in holding back: There's too much out there. And, we often found that each new road is prettier than the next. So, in the process of route finding, we have asked ourselves the following questions again and again. Do we end it here? Do we use that *other* road too? How long should we make this tour? In general, these tours are half-day rides for the average cyclist, those whom we perceive as not having a great deal of time but having an interest in exploring other aspects of a new place.

It may help you to know how we discovered, researched, and finally settled on the tours in this book. Each was a little parable of life—sometimes they came together flawlessly, others were more difficult, some were abandoned, and a few were cursed. First we studied maps of the areas we found most interesting, and that we felt had the highest scenic value. Then it was a question of the roads themselves. We tried to use quiet back roads as much as possible, exercising a cautious prejudice against county roads. But, in the process, we discovered the vast differences in the county roads we covered. Some behave like state highways, crammed with white-knuckled, heedless drivers, while others are very quiet and, in fact, idyllic (some are even dirt). These county roads are not only inconsistent in character within each county, they are not always consistent within themselves (and especially where they cross county lines). Some are flat-out dangerous, where for some reason drivers exceed the speed limit. Others are little-used, meandering roads—even in populated areas. The thing is, county roads in general tend to have excellent riding surfaces and open views of the surrounding country, but they don't always have shoulders, and most cyclists feel that such roads are not desirable for touring.

When we decided upon an area to research, we looked for a village with a post office, which usually (but not always) means there's a town park or municipal lot nearby. It never occurred to us that public access (i.e., a suitable, off-street parking area) would be an issue, but it can be, even in rural areas. Often, there was a state park or multi-use area nearby, so some of the tours begin in remote areas. (Plan ahead, in such cases, for last minute needs.) Then we looked at the open space between the county roads, at the back roads, the mecca of modern-day cyclists. Within these we contrived a loop or, in cases where the scenery or conditions are exceptional, an out-and-back spur joined to a loop. Since this is done using county maps without contour lines for the most part, we paid little attention to elevation. (You like hills, don't you?) This doesn't make as much difference in the Eastern Hudson Valley (we're thinking of exceptions and Bash Bish comes to mind) as it does in the Catskills. Accordingly, we don't discuss hills unless there's a memorable one. Suffice it to say that Columbia and Dutchess counties are hilly, the Catskills are mountainous, and the Gunks are both.

When we found a loop, we explored it, taking care to avoid offensive county roads. It was inevitable that some of them are used for connections and shortcuts. And in some areas of the Valley, or when it was really worth it, we used more of them (and a few longer rides are almost all on county roads). There are a few miles of riding on state roads as well, but these are limited. We have been careful not to use obviously fast, busy roads with soft or nonexistent shoulders. The problem with all of this figuring and fudging is that some riders will be unfazed by a given road while others will feel uncomfortable with it. We've tried to keep this in mind, and we let you know it up front. On some of the rides, you have to toe the line and hug the shoulder. On others you can ride for miles in a daze. We try to tell you the difference. But keep in mind that we're reporting on conditions we experienced on our own rides, and that you may find them very different when you take yours.

Once we established a loop in a town that we felt was of interest, we tried to identify other possibilities. Can the average rider finish this tour and still have time to look around the area? Will the serious rider want more miles or not care about the area beyond the tour itself? With many of the tours we tried to fashion two or more loops. Obviously, there's so much out there that many of these little loops act only as an introduction of sorts to any given area. Then, to get more miles, all you have to do is look at a county map and go. In this manner, we've endeavored to weed out the good from the so-so. It's hard to look at a map and arbitrarily decide on a riding destination. As residents of the Mid-Hudson Valley, we've tried to bring you to what we feel are the best general riding areas to get you started. Are there ones we've missed? Inevitably. But we feel we've included all of the regional scenic destinations with rides that will exhibit their finest assets. Every guide-book is a resource on which to build, their major function being to help you maximize your time afield in the beautiful places you may not have stumbled upon on your own.

The tragedy of writing this kind of a book is that you can't see it all. (Actually that's not true. If you were to quit your job and become a latter-day nomad, you could ride every road in all of the counties we cover—but you better get started now.) You just have to trust that what you're seeing and riding is representative of most of the mileage that's out there. Then, when you get to the end of the ride, there's always more. Right over that hill, down in that hollow, along that ridge, across that plains. You don't have to think of it as tragic; just think that the end is simply another beginning, because it is.

MEASURING MILES AND CUMULATIVE ELEVATION Don't get too up-set when our mileage doesn't match your own, because in most cases, it won't. Not that it'll be far off, but it won't always coincide. Our bicycles are equipped with cyclometers (odometers) that measure miles in both tenths and hundredths. And why, one may wonder, do they put a hundredth space on a cyclometer? Because they can. You sure don't need it. But for the benefit of those who have such devices, we have not endeavored to reconcile our hundredths back into tenths. What-ever our own odometers said, we've generally stuck with it. Your miles ought to match ours, generally speaking, within a few clicks. Sometimes your tenths will, but your hundredths? Maybe never. And, has your odometer been calibrated accurately? Shop calibrations are reliable, in general, but they can be way off, too. We have corrected (adjusted) our mileage using seamless USGS topographic maps on CD-ROM and have found this to be the most accurate way to measure miles. (These are also rendered in hundredths.) Your miles won't be as important as a close attention to the route, that is, watching for the right road and taking the right turn. We're aware, of course, that some riders don't have odometers on their bikes and don't want them, a choice that makes any discussion of mileage purely anecdotal.

ELEVATION You rarely if ever see cumulative elevation gain in a bike tour description. Such things are related more to foot travel in moun-tainous country. And while such information is useful to the cyclist as well, cumulative gain is difficult to calculate without the aid of an electronic mapping program. Establishing simple vertical rise is easy— you simply compare the highest elevation to the lowest. But vertical rise determined in this manner does not include all of the little rises and dips that you encounter along the way between the highest and lowest points. (There is more of this kind of terrain in cycling than there is in hiking because day hiking, in particular, tends to be along the line of a continuous rise to a given high point, like a mountain). Cumulative elevation reflects all of the uphill travel involved in a circuitous or linear route. Why is this information of use to a cyclist? For one, it establishes an elevation profile that can be interpreted linearly, which will help you to determine the trip's difficulty. Linear elevation profiles are exagger-ated in terms of steepness because the

X-axis (miles) can't easily be shown in accurate relation to the Y-axis (feet).

You may, for example, be up for a 15-mile flatland tour, but are you in the mood for the same tour with say, a cumulative mile or more of elevation gain? That's a lot of hills. So with a little experience, you'll be able to look at a tour and judge whether it's relatively flat or pretty hilly by comparing miles to cumulative gain in feet. How difficult that ratio is depends on the tour's length and your fitness level.

MAPS County maps are your best bet by far for navigating all of the tours in this book. They are also the most locally available. But you can also use USGS topographical maps in almost any scale, except that these become costly and impractical in detailed coverage. And you don't need that kind of detail for a bike tour. We have, at times, used USGS 1:100,000 scale, metric 30x60 minute maps that cover large areas. All of these (the coverage for New York State) are compiled from 1:24,000 scale maps dated from 1945–1980. Thus, road changes made in the last 25 years may not be evident.

So again, county maps are the most up-to-date, the cheapest, and probably the most reliable maps for your purpose. The inserts of village and city streets on county maps are also useful. What we feel is missing in these maps are the details we all like to see: topography—woodland and named water features. And because geographical literacy (i.e., knowing what you're looking at) is part of appreciating any kind of touring, with the use of a county map you may find yourself at a loss.

The tours in this book were developed from county maps. But even the best maps can't keep up with changes on the ground, especially in places like Dutchess and Columbia counties, where open space is being swallowed up rapidly. Things are a little different in the Catskills, where large, long-established parcels of state land tend to defy change. If you stick to the main route, you're fine. But if you want to get creative, bear in mind that among the smaller roads you see on the (county) maps, especially ones that you may want to use for an extension or shortcut, some may no longer exist. And if you've gone out of your way to discover that (as we have done many times), you might be inconvenienced, delayed, or caught in the dark.

The maps in this book are designed to get you through the route without depending on other resources. However, it is never wise to depend on only one source, and it is more interesting to have a few different maps. Also, should you choose to bail out or reroute the tour, you'll need an accurate reference map. Finally, you're going to need a county map, *New York Atlas & Gazetteer,* or state road map to navigate to the tour's starting place. So come prepared!

WHAT TO BRING   Of the three most important things to bring along for a comfortable and enjoyable tour, the first things that come to our minds are layers—including a waterproof one. Next comes the tools and ability to fix a flat. The third item is food.

We can't stress the first one enough. Even though breathable waterproof outerwear (like Gore-Tex) is expensive these days, there really is nothing like it. Unlike other sorts of raingear that don't breath while keeping you dry, you can wear breathable, waterproof clothing for plain-old protection from wind and cold, just as you would any other garment. And so, although it may be more costly, a quality waterproof outer layer is all-purpose. Get the highest quality rainwear you can afford and always carry at least the top. In cooler weather, carry a full suit. Carry a waterproof cap if your jacket doesn't have a hood, one that you can contrive to wear under your helmet (such as a short-brimmed hat worn backwards).

The ability to fix a flat is vital. This simple task can often be completed with just a patch in less than 10 minutes, but a good blowout might necessitate a new tube. If you're far from your car without either, you could be in for a very long walk. Carry a new replacement tube, a tire repair kit, and a pump that's easy to operate (not all pumps are created equal—some are actually useless). In addition to a pump, we carry a CO_2 inflator, which after a little practice will win your heart. You can also get foam (like the fix-a-flat used for autos) to use on a slow leak. Whatever you do, learn to fix flats. It's an easy but often dirty job, so bring a moist towelette for cleanup.

A simple, nourishing lunch is not only a necessity for people who spend the day cycling—it's a morale builder. Bring along a good sandwich and a variety of fruit and energy bars or the gel packs that endurance athletes and racers use (even though sucking gel is an unnatural act that will make you feel insect-like). Leave a few energy bars in your bike bag and forget about them—they'll come in handy for last minute rides where you've neglected to pack extra calories. We often overlook the fact that bike touring is demanding, physical work. Having a lunch with you focuses your attention on a place where you can stop and relax, too—in a wooded park or along the edge of a stream or on a grassy hillside. You can take the time to really enjoy yourself while keeping your energy level topped off.

START PACKING WITH A HANDY CHECKLIST FOR ESSENTIALS

- Full water bottles or backpack hydration system
- Cycling shorts
- Helmet
- Sunglasses
- Gloves
- First-aid kit
- Matches
- Lock
- Tire-repair tools and patch kit
- Pump or inflator
- Spare tube
- Basic tool kit or multi tool
- Maps and compass
- Lunch and snacks
- Sunscreen
- Insect repellant
- Raingear
- Headlamp/batteries

BICYCLE SAFETY Statistics have shown that the use of a bicycle helmet will almost eliminate your chances of receiving a head injury (by 85 percent, anyway, according to the Bicycle Helmet Safety Institute). So why not wear one? Also, the use of a helmet will help you ride more confidently and will protect you from the other guy. Children under 16 years of age are required to wear helmets in New York State, but it makes sense for everyone to do so.

Remember that you're riding on pretty roads, where scenery is at a premium. Keep your eye on the road, and stay to the right. Auto drivers will be looking at the scenery, too, so be aware of this and drive defensively. Ride the shoulder if you can do so comfortably, and keep to the white line on the right (the fog line) when there's no shoulder, or a very soft one.

Dress in bright clothing, the kind they make for cyclists, and ride in the same direction as the traffic. Signal your intentions plainly to motorists and hold your ground, but don't take up half of the lane.

When you're riding in a town, walk your bike on the pedestrian crosswalks. Don't ride on the sidewalks in the middle of town, and never ride the sidewalk around a corner. Be extremely cautious at intersections, observing the fact that most bicycle/car-related accidents take place here. (Remember too, that the largest portion of the American driving public is getting older.)

INTERNATIONAL MOUNTAIN BIKING ASSOCIATION (IMBA) RULES OF THE TRAIL You won't be riding on roads all the time, so it will be helpful to review the IMBA trail rules and apply the same level of courtesy toward people, animals, and the environment in all of your bicycling.

• Ride on open trails only
• Leave no trace
• Control your bicycle
• Always yield the trail
• Never spook animals
• Always plan ahead

BEFORE YOU GO Every year, begin your cycling season with a checkup by a trained shop mechanic or other qualified person. Then, before every ride, follow up with your own inspection and adjustment of the tire pressure, brakes and pads, and brake and derailleur cables. Use a quality synthetic chain lubricant on your chain and cluster. Properly adjust your seat and carefully attach your bar bag, rack pack, or panniers. Go through this exercise time and again throughout the season and on individual rides, especially when you are about to descend a long, steep hill.

MID-HUDSON BICYCLE CLUB (MHBC) The MHBC, the most active cycling club in the Mid-Hudson Valley, was founded in 1966. It offers organized rides and activities to anyone interested in cycling, from beginner to expert. The MHBC posts a ride calendar that includes weekend and weeknight training rides. Write to info@midhudson bicycle.org.

I. WEST OF THE HUDSON

The Alfred K. Smiley Memorial Tower (Sky Top) in the Mohonk Preserve

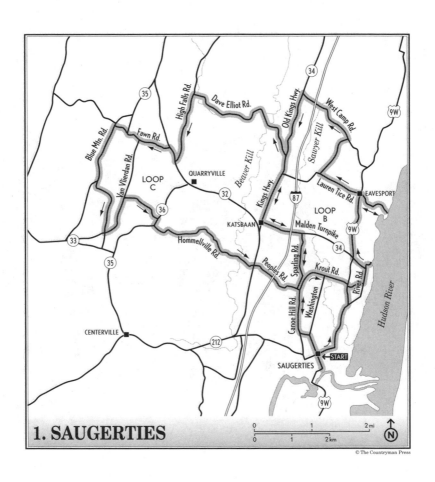

1. SAUGERTIES

The Catskills

1

De Zaagertjes: Saugerties

DISTANCE: Loop B, 14 miles; Loop C, 18 miles

CUMULATIVE ELEVATION GAIN: Loop B, 628 feet; Loop C, 925 feet

TERRAIN: Hilly

DIFFICULTY: Loop B, easy; Loop C, moderate

RECOMMENDED BICYCLE: Mountain, hybrid, road

DIRECTIONS

Saugerties is off Exit 20 of the New York State Thruway (I-87). As you leave the northbound exit, turn right; and as you leave the southbound exit, make two successive left-hand turns. This will put you on Ulster Avenue (NY 32 south, US 9W south) heading into the village. At the corner of Market Street and Ulster Avenue, bear right, then turn left onto Main Street. At the next light, turn right on Partition Street. Go a half block and turn left at the sign designating the municipal parking lot.

The marked and designated bike routes of Saugerties are testimony to what two determined citizens (and regular guys) can do for their community. Gil Hales and Mike Harkavy, both active cyclists and residents of this scenic riverside town, decided that Saugerties ought to have a bike route or two. Neither served on the town board or planning committee, nor did they have any expertise in the area of bike route development. What they did see was the creation of designated bicycle routes in nearby towns (such as Rhinebeck). And with the benefit of their experiences, they set about their mission of establishing three routes in their hometown of Saugerties. Three years later, they accomplished that mission with the help of several organizations such as the Greenway Conservancy, Scenic Hudson, and the Winnakee Land Trust (not to mention the village and town of Saugerties). Today, Saugerties has three bike routes, each marked with distinctive green-on-white state bicycle touring signs, and can rightly be called a heritage touring destination.

"There are always local political hurdles," Mike and Gil are quick to point out, "but the overall process went easily, from getting a Greenway grant to creating a brochure." The two envisaged what many regional planners see as a series of loops connecting the river towns in a linear fashion, reflecting the Greenway concept of providing recreational links between the historic and scenic areas of the valley. Mike and Gil have a futuristic plan as well. "What we really hope to see from this is that local governments will start to look at bicycles as a viable means of transportation and create more shared roadways and accommodation for cycling traffic." Amen.

Included here are the two longer loops, B and C. Loop A (The Historic Village Bike Route) is not included in the text. "The Saugerties Scenic/ Historic Bike Routes" brochure created by Barbara Bravo is available at several locations in town, including the village and town offices and tourist center. It details points of interest that are not included here, as well as three maps and photos. (Note: Mileage between this text and the brochure will differ slightly.)

Saugerties (De Zaagertjes, the Sawyers, 1663) was an early sawmill town and shipping port. Today it is a den of antiquity, where you'll enjoy spending the day at the various shops and eateries. Saugerties is also the homeport of the sloop *Clearwater* and was the site of the Woodstock Festival in 1994.

Note: As you ride, pay attention to the text, as parts of the loops overlap and it's easy to get confused by relying totally on the map.

THE HUDSON RIVER ROUTE (LOOP B)

0.00 Turn left out of the municipal parking lot onto Russell Street.

0.10 Turn left on Washington Avenue.

0.22 Cross Main Street.

0.70 Pass Cantine Field and the entrance to Saugerties High School.

1.65 Bear right on Kraut (a.k.a. Krout) Road and ascend to the intersection of US 9W.

2.10 Turn right on US 9W (use caution—it's busy) and take an immediate left off US 9W onto Fiero Road. Follow the bike signs to River Road.

2.40 Cross CR 34 (Malden Turnpike).

2.56 Turn left on River Road, and then bear right onto Riverside Drive.

2.85 Arrive at Malden Riverside Park. Upon leaving the park, turn right on River Road and ride to the stop sign, where you'll join Malden Turnpike. At the corner of the park to your left, you will see a memorial to the battleship Maine, sunk in 1898.

3.10 Continue straight ahead on Malden Turnpike to its intersection with US 9W.

3.15 Turn right on US 9W. Use caution.

4.25 Turn right on Emerick Road and descend, crossing the New York Central railroad tracks. Emerick Road becomes Eavesport Road. Descend.

5.00 Arrive at the state park at Eve's Point on the Hudson River. Retrace your steps to US 9W.

5.60 Cross US 9W onto Lauren Tice Road.

6.40 Turn right onto John Shultz (a.k.a. John Shults) Road.

7.20 Turn left on West Camp Road.

7.60 Pass the Great Vly on your right, a large wetland and important migratory waterfowl habitat. The Department of Environmental Conservation (DEC) has provided an access road (ahead on right), but you can't get too close to the water.

7.94 Pass the Vly Access Road.

8.10 Cross the New York State Thruway (I-87) overpass.

8.35 Turn left on Old Kings Highway at Asbury Corners.

9.90 Pass the Katsbaan Church and continue to the four-way intersection (Malden Four Corners).

10.70 At Malden Four Corners in Katsbaan, turn left on Malden Turnpike.

11.20 Cross the Thruway bridge. Turn right on Sparling Road and ride to its end.

12.40 Turn left and cross the railroad tracks onto Canoe Hill Road.

12.45 Turn right on Canoe Hill Road and continue to the Cantine Field entrance (Bob Moser Road).

13.10 Turn left on Bob Moser Road.

13.25 Turn right onto Washington Avenue.

14.00 Turn right on Russell Street and ride to the municipal parking lot.

THE MOUNTAIN VIEW BIKE ROUTE (LOOP C)

0.00 From the municipal parking lot on Russell Street, turn left on Russell Street and continue to Washington Avenue.

0.10 Turn left on Washington Avenue.

0.20 Cross Main Street and continue to Bob Moser Road at Cantine Field.

0.65 Turn left on Bob Moser Road and go through Cantine Field to Market Street.

0.90 Turn right on Market Street, which becomes Canoe Hill Road as you pass North Street.

1.55 Turn left and cross the railroad tracks and make an immediate right onto Sparling Road.

2.55 Turn left on Malden Turnpike (CR 34).

3.25 Turn right on Old Kings Highway.

4.10 Pass the Katsbaan Church on your left.
This is Saugerties' oldest church, which was built in 1732 and rebuilt in 1867. The names of the builders are etched into stones that form part of the north wall. Katsbaan (originally "Kaatsbaan") was the site of a Native American lacrosse field. A Dutch farmstead existed here from 1690.

4.50 Turn left on Dave Elliot Road. As you descend to the Beaverkill, you're treated to views of the Indian Head Wilderness Area on your left. Cross the creek and climb. Beyond the gravel pit the road turns rural. Pass a wetland on your left amid the hemlock shaded Beaver Kill.

6.80 Turn left on High Falls Road.

8.00 Turn right on NY 32. Traffic is heavy but the shoulder is good. Stay to the right.

8.30 Turn left on Fawn Road.

9.40 Turn left onto Blue Mountain Road (CR 35). Again, the scenery of the high eastern escarpment greets you.

11.80 Turn left onto Reservoir Road and proceed over the bridge past the Saugerties Village Reservoir, bearing left onto Clark Van Vlierdan Road (a.k.a. Van Vierdan).

12.50 Turn right on Brink Road and climb.

13.25 Turn right on Harry Wells Road (CR 36).

13.40 Turn left on Hommellville Road and ascend, then descend a long and winding road with a loose surface. You'll cross the Beaver Kill again as the descent levels out.

15.50 Cross NY 32 (be careful—it's busy and fast and this is a dangerous corner) onto Peoples Road. Cross the railroad tracks again and turn right onto Canoe Hill Road. Turn left into the Cantine Field entrance on Bob Moser Road.

17.25 Bear right onto Washington Avenue and retrace your route to Russell Street.

17.85 Turn right and ride to the municipal parking lot.

18.00 Arrive at the parking lot.

2

Beyond the Great Vly: High Falls

DISTANCE: 27.5 miles

CUMULATIVE ELEVATION GAIN: 1825 feet

TERRAIN: Hilly

DIFFICULTY: Strenuous

RECOMMENDED BICYCLE: Mountain, hybrid, road

DIRECTIONS

From the traffic light at the corner of NY 212 and NY 32, set to zero and drive north on NY 32. At 1.8 miles turn right onto CR 34 (Old Kings Highway). At 2.8 miles, pass the Old Dutch Church and Total Tennis on your left. Continue to the next crossroad at 4.15 miles and turn right on West Camp Road. Soon after crossing over the NYS thruway (I-87), slow down. At 4.5 miles, look carefully on the left for the WILDLIFE MANAGEMENT AREA (WMA) signs on the trees on either side of two wooden posts. Follow the dirt road about 400 feet to its end, where there's a small parking space, used mostly by paddlers and duck hunters. Come back out of the parking lot and turn right on West Camp Road to begin.

Where the farmlands abutted the wilderness at the base of the Catskill Escarpment (as they do to this day), the earliest route to the Catskill Mountain House threaded its way across the Kaaterskill Valley. Weekend visitors with their steamer trunks and wide-brimmed sun hats came by steamboat to Catskill Landing, where they were packed into carriages for the 10-mile ride up The Long Level and Dead Ox Hill to Pine Orchard. They came by the route that is still called the

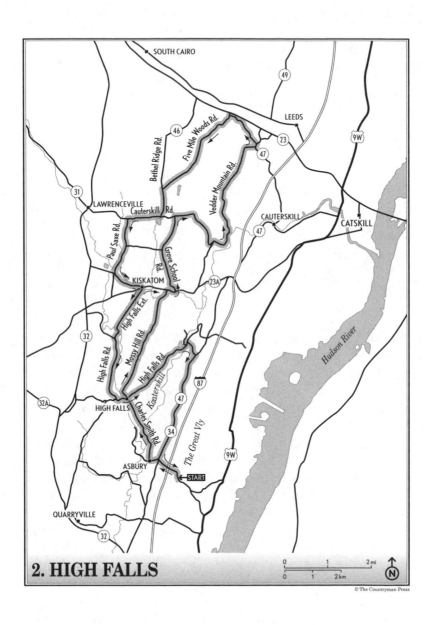

2. HIGH FALLS

Mountain Turnpike today (at the point where it enters the forest preserve, Saxe's Road is a foot and horse trail that goes to North Lake) and began the ascent up the Escarpment headwall at Saxe's Farm. You will still see allusions of this gateway to the Catskills on local maps and historic signs, and you may even feel the same sentiments that the visitors of the early 1800s felt as they saw the great Catskills rising from the low Kiskatom Flats—sublimation.

0.00 Come out of the Great Vly WMA parking area and turn right.

0.20 Cross the I-87 overpass.

0.50 Turn right on Kings Highway (CR 34). Jog left immediately onto School House Road.

A state historic sign says that troops from the Battle of Saratoga were greeted here, fed, and escorted down the Kings Road by joyous townspeople. The house on this corner was long ago a sanatorium for tubercular children.

0.70 Turn right onto C (Charles) Smith Road. The road is unlined and paved, with a low dirt shoulder.

1.15 Cross the Kaaterskill Creek at the site of an old Dutch homestead. Ascend.

2.30 Follow Mossy Hill Road to the north, keeping the creek on your left.

This is a beautiful spot, especially when the Kaaterskill is running high. At the intersection in High Falls, take some time to look downstream at the high sedimentary rocks of High Falls Gorge on the Kaaterskill Creek. Unfortunately, the falls is on private land. This is the site of the old Camp Rip Van Winkle (private). Many camp cottages and houses remain to the northeast along High Falls Road (your return route).

On Mossy Hill Road, you will pass by the old houses and cottages of Camp On-Ti-Ora (from Henry Rowe Schoolcraft's manufactured place-name for the Catskills, Onteora, or Land in the Sky). The area is heavily wooded. There are good views of the Catskill Escarpment and the Catskill Mountains to your left.

Following a deep hemlock woods and wetland, arrive at NY 23A.

5.20 At NY 23A, turn right. There's a 2-foot hard shoulder. This road can be busy, so stay right. Descend. Signal and use caution as you prepare to turn left.

5.30 Turn left and ascend on Grove School Road.

6.00 Pass Grove School Farm on the right.

6.60 Pass Ufferts Road on the left. You can shortcut the trip here by turning left to Paul Saxe Road (see mile 17.3 in that case). Continue straight ahead.

7.25 Turn right on Cauterskill Road. Ride downhill, through an area of farmsteads and open fields. Ride next to Kaaterskill Creek for a short distance, as the road becomes Cauterskill Creek Road.

9.30 Turn left on Vedder Mountain Road and climb.

10.00 Climb steeply. Vedder Mountain's east slopes rise sharply to the left. To the right there are open fields and juniper thickets. Pass a picturesque dairy farm in a stand of mature Norway spruce.

11.75 Turn left on CR 47. There's a centerline but no shoulders.

11.80 Turn left onto Vedder Road. Pass the Old Katskill Gatehouse (private, 1729).

There was a Native American village here prior to the homestead, possibly the dwelling place of the chief named Kiskataam, also the township's namesake. The barn was built in 1680 (gone).

Ascend now.

12.80 Go left on Five Mile Woods Road. This is a patched road with a vague centerline and no shoulder. You'll pass through an ugly residential area now.

15.30 Turn left onto Bethel Ridge Road (unlined, soft shoulder).

15.90 Turn right onto Cauterskill Road.

16.70 Turn left onto Paul Saxe Road (unmarked). Sunrise Farm is on your right.

There are extraordinary views of the eastern Catskills here, from North Mountain down to Overlook Mountain. You're looking out over the Kiskatom Flats, once the bottom of glacial Lake Kiskatom.

17.30 Pass Ufferts Road (the shortcut road) on your left.

High Falls Gorge, running high

18.00 Turn left at the intersection of Paul Saxe Road and Ramsey School Road onto Mountain Turnpike Road.

18.80 Bear left and diagonally cross NY 23A and turn right onto High Falls Road Extension.

20.20 Cross the Kaaterskill Creek at a falls and the site of an old mill. The millpond dam is breached at its midpoint.

20.30 Bear left onto High Falls Road. Bear left at Nelson Hoff Road and descend to High Falls again.

22.00 Continue northeast on High Falls Road. Pass an emerging wetland and beaver pond on the left. This is a narrow, paved, and scenic two-lane road.

24.00 Cross the Kaaterskill Creek as it winds its way north. Climb now.

24.40 Turn right onto Kings Highway (CR 47). This is a lined road with poor or absent shoulders. Traffic can be brisk, but it's local and seems fairly bike savvy. The speed limit is 45 mph. Enjoy the scenery of the Catskills to your right. The road changes to CR 34 as you enter Ulster County.

27.00 Arrive at the corner of School House Road and West Camp Road, which you'll recognize. Turn left onto West Camp Road.

27.50 Turn left into the Great Vly WMA parking area.

3

Zanzibar: The Great Eastern Cloves

DISTANCE: 20.6 miles

CUMULATIVE ELEVATION GAIN: 2700 feet

TERRAIN: Very steep hills

DIFFICULTY: Strenuous

RECOMMENDED BICYCLE: Mountain, hybrid, road

DIRECTIONS

From Saugerties Exit 20 off the New York State Thruway (I-87), follow NY 32 north, 6 miles to NY 32A and turn left toward Palenville. Arrive in Palenville at 8 miles and bear left onto NY 23A. Go 0.5 mile to the forest preserve access parking lot on the right, just before entering the Catskill Park (sign posted).

This tour begins in the eastern Catskills tannery and bluestone town of Palenville, which sits at the bottom of Kaaterskill Falls, and rides a circle around the Kaaterskill Wild Forest. You begin with a more or less level cruise along a flat glacial lake bottom (Lake Kiskatom) below the Escarpment, the ridge that separates the valley from the high dissected plateau of the eastern Catskills. The route then turns west to climb what was is probably the single most romanticized landscape feature in 19th-century America (Platte Clove)—with the exception of the nearby Kaaterskill Falls and Pine Orchard area. This is a challenging, scenic hill climb that finishes with a dreamlike descent through Kaaterskill Clove.

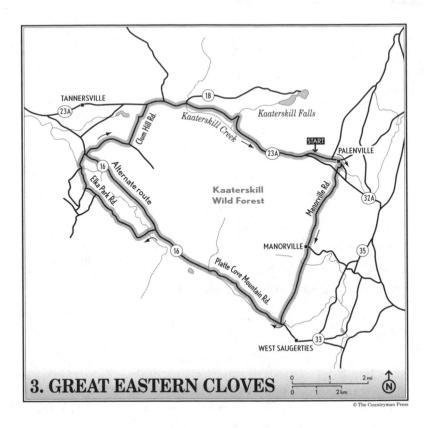

3. GREAT EASTERN CLOVES

© The Countryman Press

0.00 From the forest preserve access parking lot, head back into Palenville along NY 23A.

0.50 Bear right on NY 32A and immediately right onto Pine Avenue.

0.70 Bear right onto Woodstock Avenue (a.k.a. Manorville Road). Continue straight ahead, as Woodstock Avenue officially becomes Manorville Road.

5.25 Turn right onto CR 33, which becomes Platte Clove Mountain Road. Your elevation gain to this point has been less than 300 feet, but that's all about to change.

6.00 At the bottom of Platte Clove, the road rises suddenly and steeply. There is a SEASONAL USE ONLY road sign posted here, warning that the road is closed from April through November. There are no lines or shoulders. Traffic is minimal

Looking east into the Hudson Valley from the upper elevations of Platte Clove

and cautious, but because the *long* way down the mountain through Kaaterskill Clove is the nearest alternate route into the valley from Hunter, a small number of commuters use this road. Many motorists are indeed afraid to travel this road even under ideal conditions. Now you will engage upon the 1,200-foot climb to the top of the Clove.

Steep ledges rise to the right, and a deep canyon develops to your left. See if you can find The Eye, a mysterious, football field–sized sculpture by Kevin VanHentenryck. Look in the north wall of rock along the road. Soon you will come to a scenic bend in the road. When the water table is high, you may have a look at one or two waterfalls that represent the remnant streams that carved this impressive ravine some 15 thousand years ago. With a quick study of the surrounding geology, you'll notice that the mountain is continuously falling into the Clove at this point, requiring constant maintenance to keep it open. As you gain elevation beyond the bend, views of the Hudson Valley appear to the southeast.

Platte Clove was widely popularized in Lionel DeLisser's Picturesque Catskills
(Greene County), *published in 1894. DeLisser roamed the countryside with his cumbersome dry plate camera equipment in a carriage drawn by a horse named Cherry Tree. His illustrations include many that were taken in the heart of Platte Clove, where a series of waterfalls on state land are now enclosed by private property.*

8.00 At the top of Platte Clove, you will pass the Kaaterskill Wild Forest parking area on the right.

This is part of the Long Path, a trail that stretches from the George Washington Bridge to the Helderbergs. The first house on your left is the little, red, artist-in-residence cabin belonging to the Catskill Center for Conservation and Development (CCCD) in Arkville, New York. If you've got a few minutes, you can lean your bike against a tree and take the trail that leads from the cabin a short way downhill to beautiful Plattekill Falls, a 10-minute hike. The CCCD has asked that people do not disturb the artist in residence.

This rugged landscape is the region through which Revolutionary raiding parties of Native Americans and Tories escaped to western Tory strongholds, often taking with them prisoners whom they enslaved, traded, or sold for ransom. The remnant of a Tory fort (nothing more than a small stone wall), where such parties were known to have spent their first night of retreat, can still be seen low down on the southern slopes of Roundtop Mountain.

9.50 Turn left onto Dale Lane. Note: There is a dirt section on this part of the ride that can be avoided by continuing on Platte Clove Road (CR 16), where the route is joined again at Clum Hill Road.

9.90 Turn right onto Roaring Kill Road.

10.20 The road becomes a seasonally maintained dirt surface.

10.60 Pass parking for the Indian Head Wilderness Area Trailhead on your left. Cross the picturesque Roaring Kill and continue.

11.60 Bear right at Mink Hollow Road onto Elka Park Road.

To the left the road leads to a dead end at the edge of state land where the old Mink Hollow Road connected Woodstock to the Tannersville-Hunter area as early as 1790.

11.80 Turn right at the Y, continuing on Elka Park Road.

12.40 Pass the Elka Park post office on the right and cross the Schoharie Creek.

12.80 Turn right on Platte Clove Road (CR 16).

Note: You can route this tour through nearby Tannersville by bearing left on CR 16 and riding 1.5 miles into town, thereafter taking NY 23A to the east 1.4 miles to rejoin the main route at mile 15.4. This would cut out the substantial hill climb over Clum Hill (380 feet, 2.6 miles) and shorten the tour by 0.3 mile. Tannersville is a colorful, interesting town with many little cafes and shops, including a bike shop.

12.85 Turn left onto Clum Hill Road and ascend.

14.25 Turn left at the T, remaining on Clum Hill Road. You're on the western fringes of the Kaaterskill Wild Forest. There are good views of the Devil's Path Range to the south. Heading north-northeast, you begin a fast descent.

15.40 At the corner of Clum Hill Road and NY 23A, turn right onto NY 23A. The road is busy at times, as this is a popular summer resort area. Keep right and drive defensively. Selena's Diner (highly recommended) is on the left at this intersection.

16.40 In Haines Falls, you are at the top of Kaaterskill Falls and will now begin the long (about 4 miles) descent down to Palenville.

This is a good time to tighten things up, check your brakes, and secure your loose items. The Twilight General Store is on the left a short distance north on CR 18 (North Lake Road, a.k.a. Mountain House Road) on the left. Don your most visible clothing, adjust your helmet straps, and shout "Geronimo."

17.90 Pass the hiker's access parking area for the Kaaterskill Falls Trailhead and continue the descent.

18.20 Go through the hairpin turn.

That's Bastion Falls on your left. Kaaterskill Falls (at 260 feet, the highest waterfall in the state) is up the marked foot trail at 0.4 mile. This is Spruce Creek. To the right, below Haines Falls (private), it becomes Kaaterskill Creek.

The descent continues. Stay to the right. The shoulder is not always useable. Be advised that there's a passing zone ahead.

The scenery is spectacular now as you freewheel into Kaaterskill Clove. You'll smell burning brakes as the cars stream past you, or shall we say "if" the cars stream past you. You'll be going pretty fast. The road surface is fair to good, but there are cracks and heaves. If you time this ride for a weekday, around midday, you may experience very little traffic, which will limit the inconvenience of road and shoulder quality and let you enjoy a safer experience. Weekends will be busy.

19.50 Cross More's Bridge.

You can get close to the creek here with your bike in sight. There are generally people swimming here on hot days. You'll pass by several more popular swimming areas ahead (where you may see cars parked), but you can't get as close to them with your bike.

There are a few level areas, where you'll actually have to pedal a little, and a tight, blind turn or two. Use caution here.

20.60 Look on the left side of the road for the forest preserve access parking area and your car.

4

All Creation, Lad: North Lake Loop

DISTANCE: 7.3 miles

CUMULATIVE ELEVATION GAIN: 200 feet

DIFFICULTY: Easy

TERRAIN: Mostly flat, some little climbs

RECOMMENDED BICYCLE: Mountain, hybrid

DIRECTIONS

From NY 23A in the village of Haines Falls, turn right onto North/ South Lake Road, where a large yellow-and-brown state sign says NORTH/SOUTH LAKE PUBLIC CAMPGROUND AND DAY-USE AREA. The store on the left (Twilight General Store) is your last provisioning point. At 2.25 miles turn right onto Scutt Road, where you'll see FOREST PRESERVE ACCESS signs. Go down the road 200 feet and turn right into the parking area for Sleepy Hollow Horse Trail and Escarpment Trail. If this lot is full, you'll have to park on the road outside the gate or inside the campground and pay the day-use fee. To ride in from Scutt Road on your bike costs a dollar.

0.00 Pull out of the lot and make a left. You'll see where the Escarpment Trail begins on the east side of the road. (This 23-mile trunk trail goes north to Windham.) At the corner, turn right, go into the main campground entrance, and stop at the gatehouse to pay up and get a map. Go straight on the campground road (don't go right, down to South Lake).

The campground speed limit is 15 mph here, but oddly enough the drivers seem to take joy in substantially exceeding it. We have no trouble yelling out "Fifteen!" at

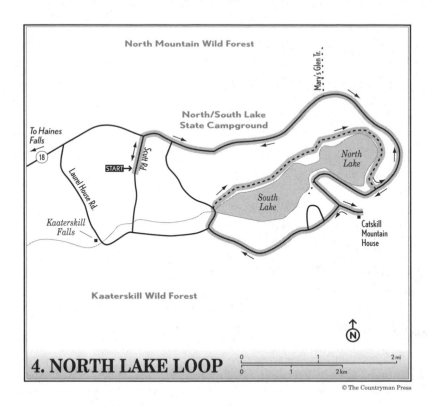

North Mountain Wild Forest

North/South Lake
State Campground

Mary's Glen Tr.

To Haines
Falls

18

START

Scutt Rd.

Laurel House Rd.

North
Lake

South
Lake

Kaaterskill
Falls

Catskill
Mountain
House

Kaaterskill Wild Forest

N

4. NORTH LAKE LOOP

0   1   2 mi
0   1   2 km

© The Countryman Press

such people, in as gruff a voice as we can muster. It rarely helps, but we feel it's
our civic duty. Many walk and ride this road with little kids.

0.80 At a stop sign go straight.

1.10 Pass the foot trail to Mary's Glen on your left.

*Said to be her favorite spot, the Glen is named for Mary Scribner. Along with her hus-
band, she ran a boarding house near Kaaterskill Falls in the mid-1800s. Thoreau visited
them in the early 1840s, but all mention of his visit was removed from the draft of Walden.
Now you see campsites and smell wood smoke.*

Soon you will arrive at the North Lake beach and picnic area.

*There are rest rooms here, and you can get water. Note how the huge white pines are all
leaning to the northeast, with their branches swept into the same direction under the in-
fluence of the prevailing winds.*

Go straight, keeping the lake close to your right and pass through a barrier gate, which may be open. Ride along the old, broken, tar road next to the lake. *The beautiful backdrop of high hills in the north includes Sunset Point and North Mountain, which the Escarpment Trail crosses. Sunset Rock is probably the most popular short hike in the eastern Catskills.*

2.20 Arrive at the narrows between North and South Lakes. This is also a snow-mobile trail, so you'll see orange or red markers. Bear left around the narrows and follow the path straight ahead (don't take the footpath that goes off to South Lake on your right). *You'll crank uphill easily past Whale Rock, where people have placed rocks (teeth) on the whale's jaws for centuries. This is a profile rock, seen in postcards for the Mountain House era that began here in 1823, with the construction of the Catskill Mountain House.*

2.50 At the South Lake picnic area parking lot, go straight ahead to a barrier gate and a sign that says CATSKILL MOUNTAIN HOUSE HISTORICAL SITE. Follow the old carriage path over rocks and gravel, climbing slightly.

2.80 Arrive at the Catskill Mountain House Historical Site, where extensive views of the Hudson Valley greet you. After a visit, turn around and retrace your tracks to the South Lake parking area. Leaving the pavilion to your right, stay on the paved road that climbs a bit before descending to the dam at the bottom of South Lake. *Look at the old rock carvings in the ledges here, with some quality etchings dating from the early to mid-1800s, plus a number of more recent and poorly done graffiti. The Escarpment Trail crosses this flat and continues north. This spot is the infamous Pine Orchard. The ledge is generally recognized as the one from which James Fenimore Cooper's peripatetic nimrod, Natty Bumppo (a.k.a. Leatherstocking or Hawkeye), issued his hackneyed and tiresome All Creation speech, an utterance that has been aped by every guidebook writer of the last two centuries—including us. (Because of his Tory allegiances, Cooper was never fully recognized as a genuinely American writer, and his popularity was often resented.)*

4.00 Cross the earthen dam at the south end of South Lake. (The fact that it's a dam isn't entirely obvious.) Turn right at the lake's edge, next to the map kiosk, go through a barrier gate, and follow the path (bikes allowed). *This is a very pretty path with views of the lake. Walkers use the path too. Yield the right-of-way.*

4.50 Join the paved service road. Continue bearing right, leaving a cabin and maintenance building to your left. A short, dead-end path to the right leads to the narrows at this point.

4.60 Turn right at the sign for CAMPSITES 0–25, following a path close to the lake.

4.70 Turn right after campsite 5, and you'll see a sign marked FOOT TRAIL. Follow it, bikes use it. Take your time.

4.90 Cross a stone bridge and enter a campsite loop. Merge with the loop at campsite 142. There are good views of Kaaterskill High Peak and Roundtop here. This is the vantage point from which Thomas Cole painted *Lake with Dead Trees* (1825), one of his early blockbusters. Be alert and observe the campsite numbers. Don't be surprised if you get lost. You can easily find your way by bearing along through the campsite loops with North Lake to your right and the service road to your left. The path is sometimes identified; other times, not. Use your intuition. Immediately following campsite 153, continue between two flat rocks where the path is once again well established.

5.10 Turn right at another loop, leaving campsite 167 to your right. At campsite 169, where it says CAMPSITES 170–171, turn right and pick up the path on a short, narrow section, where you bear right again, and again after campsite 171. Continue, watching for yellow markers, and follow the lake to the beach and picnic area. At this point, turn north and follow the North Lake campsite road back out to the main entrance.

7.30 Turn left onto Scutt Road and back to the parking area. To continue this tour to the top of Kaaterskill Falls (you can reach the bottom of the falls on foot only, and only from NY 23A), continue straight past Scutt Road instead of returning to the parking area.

7.70 Turn left onto Laurel House Road.

8.10 At the bottom of the hill, there's a stop barrier. Go around it. It's meant to keep cars out. This is not private property.

8.20 At a fork, turn right. This is part of the Laurel House carriageway system.

8.30 You'll pass a commemorative stone bench.

The stone bench is dedicated to Helen Fisk Robertson of Hartwick College, who died in an accident here at the falls. Be very careful as you approach the impacted soil around the falls ahead. Leave your bike and walk over to the falls area, where you will meet several other sightseers enjoying the views. Stay back from the precipice and avoid the slippery streambed—Kaaterskill Falls is higher than Niagara Falls and drops in two separate tiers, amounting to 260 feet.

Return the way you came.

5

Huck and the Huckleberry: Tannersville

DISTANCE: 12 miles

CUMULATIVE ELEVATION GAIN: 1300 feet

TERRAIN: Hilly

DIFFICULTY: Moderate

RECOMMENDED BICYCLE: Mountain, hybrid, road (one short dirt section)

DIRECTIONS

From the corner of NY 23A and CR 23C in Tannersville (at the only light in town), turn south on Railroad Avenue. At 0.3 mile, Railroad Avenue meets South Main Street. Ahead on the left you will see Rip Van Winkle Park. This is also the access point for the Tannersville Rail Trail (Huckleberry Trail). You can park anywhere in the village, including the large municipal lot off Main Street, but you may find the park a better place to prepare. Also, there are rest rooms available.

Few towns can claim to be more characteristic of Catskill Mountain culture and scenery than present-day Tannersville. It's ironic that this should be so, since the town derives its name from the tanning industry that was so ruinous to the natural environment. To tan a single hide, about a cord of hemlock bark was needed (roughly one tree per tanned hide). After the trees were debarked, they were left in the forest to rot. Not only did this practice eventually denude the hills of hemlocks, but it also poisoned the watershed with tannic acid. The tanning industry flourished in the Catskills from the late 1800s to the early 1900s. Hides were shipped to the Catskills from Argentina and brought to the tanneries by steamer and freight wagon. A good deal of the leather was

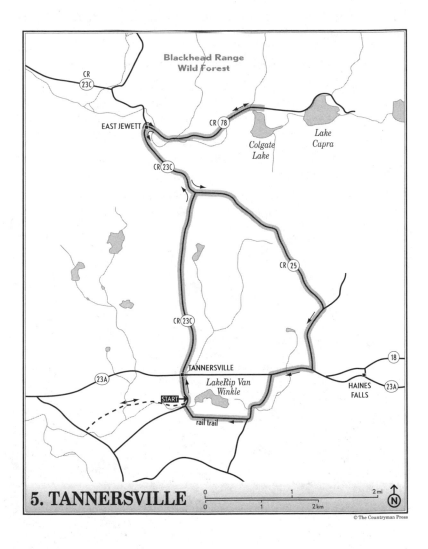

5. TANNERSVILLE

© The Countryman Press

used for Civil War boots and saddlery. The Catskills' vast, post-glacial hemlock forests have never recovered, but you'll still see a good many of them along this forested, scenic route through one of the oldest, and certainly one of the most colorful, of the eastern Catskill villages.

0.00 Leave Rip Van Winkle Park and head north on South Main Street, jogging left onto Railroad Avenue.

0.35 From the corner of NY 23A and CR 23C in Tannersville (at the only light in town), head north (uphill) on CR 23C.

1.70 You will begin to see the old, ornate homes and spires of Onteora Park. *Onteora Park is one of the Catskills' oldest cottage communities. (There are two others in the area: Twilight Park in Haines Falls and Elka Park in Tannersville.) A wealthy New York grocer, Francis Thurber, and his sister, Candace Wheeler, founded this one. They had been regular guests at the Catskill Mountain House and eventually wanted their own piece of the Catskills. They choose wisely—the park occupies scenic lands that were once part of the great Hardenburgh Patent; Robert Livingston in particular owned these. Mark Twain spent the summer of 1890 here during the height of his fame; by this time all of his important books had been written and he traveled the world conducting public readings.*

Kaaterskill High Peak and Roundtop, from the Mountain Top Arboretum

The name Onteora derives from a fanciful place-name, coined by Henry Rowe School-craft (1793–1864), the American writer, ethnologist, and explorer who is most often credited as the founder of the Mississippi's source (there are many contenders). Among the posts of his illustrious career was his appointment as Michigan's Superintendent of Indian Affairs. He translated Native American poetry and legend and wrote extensively on their culture and religion. He even married a Chippewa princess. His term (originally Ontiora) was translated as Land in the Sky and soon became synonymous with the Catskills to such an extent that many people still claim it is the Lenape name for these mountains.

2.30 Pass Maude Adams Road and the Mountain Top Arboretum on your right.

The arboretum is open to the public (privy here). Maude Adams was a well-known ac-tress and Onteora Club celebrity who suffered from tuberculosis. She took treatments at Onteora at around the same time that Dr. Trudeau was making headway with treatments in the Saranac Lake area sanatoriums. By 1884 people had discovered the benefits of clean air. Today, there is still no cure for the disease.

The Mountain Top Arboretum is a 21-acre free public facility, created in 1977 by a pri-vate donation. The staff conducts a series of lectures and special programs and holds an annual garden fair and plant sale. Of special interest is the arboretum's chestnut project, through which they have begun to create blight-resistant chestnuts. The American chest-nut was virtually extirpated by blight in the late 1800s.

2.50 Arrive at the intersection of CR 23C and Onteora Park Road (CR 25) at the site of Onteora Chapel and cemetery.

Having climbed about 570 vertical feet at this point, you're entitled to a rest, and this is the place to take it as you survey the skyline of the Devil's Path Mountains in the Indian Head Wilderness Area to the south.

After a rest, continue straight ahead (north-northwest) on CR 23C, descending now.

3.50 Turn right (east) onto CR 78 in East Jewett and head into the scenic East Kill Valley. Views to the north of the Blackhead Range appear.

5.00 Arrive at Colgate Lake, a charming picnic spot between the Blackhead Wild Forest and the East Jewett Range. This is your turnaround point. Retrace your steps to the Onteora Chapel now.

7.40 Turn left (southeast) on CR 25. At first you ride along the south slopes of the Jewett Range, and then the road descends, with views of Kaaterskill High Peak and Roundtop in the south.

10.20 At NY 23A, turn right.

10.60 Turn left onto Clum Hill Road and pass the Cortina Valley Ski Area on your left.

11.10 Turn right onto the Tannersville Rail Trail (the Huckleberry Trail). The surface is dirt/cinder, but it is in very good condition.

12.00 Arrive back at your starting point at Rip Van Winkle Park.

To explore the Huckleberry Trail (highly recommended), continue west for another 1.2 miles to the trail's present terminus, and return the same way (adding a total of 2.4 miles to your tour). The Huckleberry was the name of the train that brought guests to the Catskill mountain houses in the Pine Orchard and Kaaterskill Falls area. The wide cinder trail follows along the edge of Gooseberry Creek, through a deep hemlock glen. The creek has the habit of washing out the geology next to the trail, so exercise due caution.

6

Fire and Rain: The Schoharie Reservoir

DISTANCE: 14.3 miles

CUMULATIVE ELEVATION GAIN: 1600 feet

TERRAIN: Hilly

DIFFICULTY: Moderate

RECOMMENDED BICYCLE: Mountain, hybrid

DIRECTIONS

From Kingston Exit 19 on the New York State Thruway (I-87), go 29 miles to CR 42 in Shandaken. Head north to Lexington. At 39 miles, turn left on NY 23A. At mile 45, pass NY 23. Go another mile into Prattsville and park in the village. Note that you can also park at the (small) Pratt's Rocks parking area, just east of town on NY 23A, and ride the 0.5 mile into Prattsville.

0.00 Just before the bridge spanning the outlet of the Schoharie Reservoir on CR 7, turn right and follow CR 7 (a.k.a. Gilboa Road, Main Street). Within the space of 3 miles, the road crosses four county lines (Greene, Delaware, Greene, and Schoharie), so don't fret too much over the road names and numbers. The views of the reservoir are disappointing here because it lies hidden so close on the left side (they will improve), but the wooded buffer zone is beautiful. You gain elevation with a few short climbs.

4.60 Where the Manor Kill joins the reservoir in West Conesville at CR 39 and CR 990V, you will cross a bridge over a little gorge. Bear left on CR 3. The road is paved and lined. Traffic seems to be easy going. The shoulder is loose dirt/gravel. You begin to get better views of the reservoir to your left now.

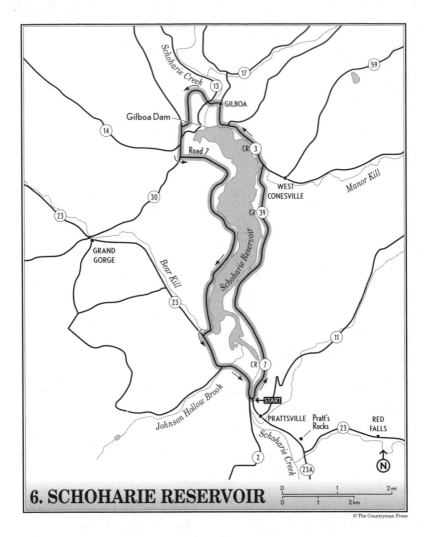

6. SCHOHARIE RESERVOIR

© The Countryman Press

5.90 Arrive at the Gilboa Dam and have a look, then continue downhill.

This 600-million-gallon-per-day impoundment has a holding capacity of 22 billion gallons and supplies the Esopus Creek and Ashokan Reservoir with New York City's drinking water. Construction began in 1917 and was finished in 1926. The sad story of the displaced Gilboa Settlement is told on a nearby information kiosk and reads like the rest of the eminent domain narratives of all the other big reservoir engineering projects in the Catskills. Gristmills, sawmills, planning mills, tanneries, 350 residents, and disinterred graves—an otherwise vibrant community—totally dismantled and then submerged. And this was not the little settlement's first encounter with calamity—the town was nearly destroyed in the flood of 1869 (the entire cotton mill and its one hundred looms were lost), and in 1890 nearly the entire town was destroyed by fire. In the 1920s there were two hotels, three churches, a creamery, theater, telegraph office, and electric company—all abandoned before the waters rose.

6.60 Pass the Department of Environmental Protection (DEP) headquarters on your left and look to the right for the Gilboa Fossils. Continue across the bridge and up the hill. It appears as if you are about to merge with a super highway, but you're not. Pass Stryker Road to the right as you climb.

Gilboa Fossils exhibits the fascinating fossilized tree ferns that were found during the impoundment's construction. The find represents the most ancient known tree species on the planet and the oldest tree fossils in existence, which grew here 370 million years ago in a tropical climate (20 degrees south of the era's equator). In 1939, Winifred Goldring, state paleontologist, called the Gilboa collection "the most known and impressive display

Heaps of driftwood form at the lip of Gilboa Dam.

of early land flora in the known world." There's a word or two about arthropods as well; the spinnerets found among these fossils are the earliest record of spiders. Oddly, though the spiders could produce silk webs, flying prey would not appear for several million years.

7.70 Turn left onto NY 30. This is not an exciting road, but it's not terrible. There's a wide shoulder. Traffic is fast and heedless. Scenery is nil. You're getting off soon, so be careful and signal your intentions.

8.30 Take Road 7 on your left; the road is a dirt one laner. The unimaginative name is a cue that you are now entering the buffer lands of the Schoharie Reservoir. Pass a horse farm.

9.40 Now you draw close to the reservoir.

You'll see many gated roads that require permits for access to the reservoir. This is the nicest part of the trip. You glide through woodlands of high quality—plantations of pine and spruce, forests of mixed hardwoods, along a dirt road where there are no residences.

12.50 Cross a bridge over the Bear Kill at the southern end of the reservoir.

12.70 Turn left onto NY 23 for more of the same treatment you had on NY 30. The shoulder is inadequate and degenerates from here, and the traffic coming into Prattsville isn't especially bike-savvy. And the good news? It's a short, mostly downhill run into town, and the closer you get, the slower the traffic goes as it enters a 35-mph speed zone.

14.30 Cross the green Bridge and ride into town to your car.

7

A Million Sides Tanned: Prattsville

DISTANCE: 15 miles

CUMULATIVE ELEVATION GAIN: 1875 feet

TERRAIN: Hilly

DIFFICULTY: Strenuous

RECOMMENDED BICYCLE: Mountain, hybrid, road

DIRECTIONS

From Kingston Exit 19 on the New York State Thruway (I-87), go 29 miles to CR 42 in Shandaken. Head north to Lexington. At 39 miles, turn left on NY 23A. At mile 45, pass NY 23. Go 0.5 mile and look carefully to your right for the Pratt's Rocks parking area.

Thoreau observed with irony that a lumberman who destroyed forests was called a model citizen, but that one who wandered in a forest for the simple sake of its beauty was called a bum. Zaddock Pratt was of the former group. He was the Catskill tanlord extraordinaire. In his lifetime he denuded more of the Catskills than any other tanner in history. For this deed, he was awarded infamy in the naming of the town (he named it himself) where he resided and operated, and that infamy is forever carved into the stone mountainside called Pratt's Rocks.

Legend has it that in 1845 Andrew Pearse, a young sculptor, was returning home to Rensselaerville when he met up with Pratt. In return for lodging, Pearse was commissioned to carve a great horse in the mountainside as part of the timeline of Pratt's life. This first carving was to reflect Pratt's love of horses—he owned over one thousand of them. Also carved in stone at the Rocks is a hemlock tree—a symbol of

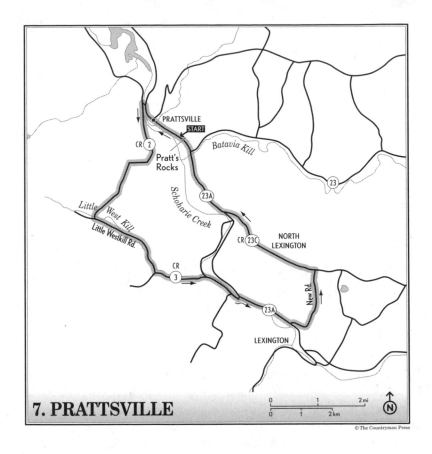

7. PRATTSVILLE

© The Countryman Press

how Pratt got his wealth. There is a more gratuitous bas-relief carved into the 350-million-year-old sandstone outcropping, for his son who died in the Civil War, and an entry of the family coat of arms and motto that read DO WELL AND DOUBT NOT. And there are others. But Pratt (1790–1871) was not totally self-serving. He served in Congress (that proves it, right?), and he was a farmer, builder, banker, and self-styled loan shark. He would even buy your barn—at a better than average price—so he could shoot it down with his canon and mock militia.

Is Pratt's curiosity graffiti or art? You can decide for yourself, as you set out on these two scenic tours amid the open hills that were once swathed in blue-green manes of shimmering hemlocks.

0.00 Leave the parking area and turn right and pedal into Prattsville (watch the traffic).

1.00 Cross the bridge over the Batavia Kill, turn left on Little Westkill Road (CR 2), and climb. This is scenic farmland. The large mountains to your right are Bear Pen and Vly. The road tops out and then descends.

3.90 CR 2 curves into the southeast and crosses the Lexington town line as it follows along the course of the Little West Kill Creek.

5.80 Turn left onto CR 3. Descend on the unlined road. There's no shoulder and limited traffic.

6.84 Turn right on West Kill Road, leaving Falke Road to your left. Ride along in full view of the Schoharie Creek on the left.

The Schoharie River from the top of Pratt's Rocks

7.80 Bear left and cross the Mosquito Point Bridge.

7.90 Turn right onto NY 23A. The shoulder is good. Stay to the right. You have views of the Schoharie Creek and the mountains.

9.30 Turn left onto New Road and ascend steeply.

10.60 Turn left on Airport Road (CR 23C). There's a centerline but no shoulder. Travel west now, through North Lexington. Eventually the centerline disappears. Far-reaching views develop. You descend steeply.

13.00 Turn right onto NY 23A. This begins with a good shoulder that deteriorates as you approach Prattsville.

14.50 Pass NY 23 on the right. Traffic is more apparent now, so be cautious as you approach the parking area at Pratt's Rocks, where the road is narrower.

15.00 Arrive at the parking area.

After securing your bikes, take some time to explore this beautiful area where Colonel Pratt built a memorial to himself. It's next to the Schoharie Creek (before it was Prattsville, this was Schoharieville). The rock carvings are only a short walk up the hill, and you've probably never seen anything like them. From certain vantage points, the carvings can be seen for many miles. There's a picnic table here where you can have your lunch beneath the shade of a few sparse hemlocks.

8

Flick's Fix: The Spruceton Valley

DISTANCE: 10 miles

CUMULATIVE ELEVATION GAIN: 650 feet

TERRAIN: Rolling

DIFFICULTY: Easy

RECOMMENDED BICYCLE: Mountain, hybrid, road (some hard dirt)

DIRECTIONS

Lexington is 8 miles west of Hunter off NY 23A. From Lexington, go south on NY 42, 4 miles to the hamlet of West Kill. Head east on CR 6, 2.8 miles to the fishing access parking area. You can add 5 miles to this tour by parking in the village of West Kill (no services). Bring your trout rod and a bathing suit.

When the Wisconsin Ice Sheet half melted/half slid off the Catskills, from which a shallow sea had long ago drained away, the soft sedimentary rocks were gouged and sculpted by glacial ice and runoff. Mastodon roamed the land, pursued by nomadic Paleo hunters, and the first evergreens appeared. Later, elk and wolves would arrive, providing food, shelter, and clothing for Early Woodland period hunter-gatherers. Fast-forward 10 thousand years: Clad in bright synthetics, a new and strange species riding on rubber tires arrived, with no apparent purpose other than to admire the natural stage where it all took place—the high and ancient valley of the West Kill. These ephemeral creatures left no trace of their presence in the thin silt; it is believed that they were transients who made their brief appearance in the Late Double-Butted Steel and Early Carbon Fiber Age.

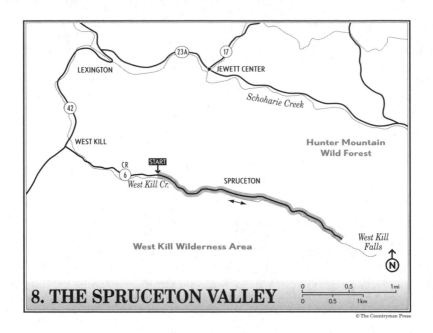

8. THE SPRUCETON VALLEY

© The Countryman Press

The high and rugged Spruceton Valley will let you feel the temporal nature of your sojourn on this spinning orb, for the landscape that you see before you has changed little since the Wisconsin Ice Sheet vaporized. And that's nothing. The base geology emerged some 200 to 300 million years before that. In other words, what you see on a tour of the West Kill Valley is a 17-thousand-year-old remodeling job of a quarter-billion-year-old house, with alpine-style window dressing, a kind of cleanup effort before the 21st-century guests would arrive.

As for recent times, life was hard for early tenant farmers in the Catskills' upper elevations because of the short growing seasons, marginal soils, heavy leases, and impatient patentees. Even today, it looks as if the local residents are just hanging on with their hobby farms. Apparently, the land's seductive charm has yielded only to fancy homes and horse farms, while the swimming pools of the old resort motels have long since filled with deep cracks and forest litter.

This is an out-and-back ride with no turns. You will be crisscrossing the West Kill, the little trout stream made famous by local resident and fly-fishing legend, Art Flick. The bible of Catskill fly-fishing is Mr. Flick's famous little *New Streamside Guide to Naturals and Their Imitations*, an anecdotal catalog and emergence schedule of the area's aquatic insects. You will probably see adult mayfly, stone fly, and caddis fly as you ride along next to the creek; they hatch throughout the summer. Because of their very poor vision, the duns often mistake the gray road for the stream in the quest to lay their eggs. If they alight on you, gently brush them off. Although they may look formidable, and in some cases a lot like an unusually colorful cockroach, they are harmless. Strong mayfly populations (and thus strong trout populations) are important indicators of a stream's health—neither can tolerate even very low levels of pollution.

0.00 Head east on CR 6. Pass the West Kill Mountain Trailhead on the right.

This is the terminus of the Devil's Path Trail, the 25-mile trunk trail that begins in Platte Clove. It is called the terminus because the trail is generally traveled east to west, the same way it was built. Known for its steep ascents and descents, Devil's Path is the region's test piece in terms of foot trails.

The road turns to dirt.

There's beautiful scenery all around you here in the settlement area of Spruceton. To the north, you can see the trailless peaks of Evergreen and Rusk Mountains in the Hunter Mountain Wild Forest. To the south, you are hemmed into a great bowl by the long line of peaks beginning with West Kill and running west over North Dome, Sherill, and Balsam in the West Kill Mountain Wilderness Area.

Pass the Spruceton Trail parking area and the trailhead for Hunter Mountain on your left. This is the Hunter Mountain Wild Forest.

4.20 Pass the overflow parking area on your right and continue on a rougher section of road that follows close to the Kill. You will have to walk your bike much of the time. (Mountain bikes are the best bet for this section.)

5.00 Arrive at West Kill Falls (a.k.a. Buttermilk Falls, Diamond Notch Falls).

This is a fairly popular destination these days; people come to sit under the waterfall during the dog days of summer. At one time the area was impacted by uncontrolled camping that led to serious abuse, but it has since been cleaned up and made off limits to camping. This trailhead leads the back way up to Hunter using the Devil's Path, while another trail heads east over the West Kill to Diamond Notch.

Return the way you came.

9

YMCA: Frost Valley

DISTANCE: 28 miles

CUMULATIVE ELEVATION GAIN: 2700 feet

TERRAIN: Rugged and mountainous

DIFFICULTY: Strenuous

RECOMMENDED BICYCLE: Mountain, hybrid, road (some dirt sections)

DIRECTIONS

From the intersection of NY 28 and CR 42 in Big Indian, bear left (south) on CR 42 (a.k.a. Slide Mountain Road). At 7.5 miles, pass the Giant Ledge parking area, and farther on, Winnisook Lake, and at 9.4 miles, the Slide Mountain Trailhead parking area. At 12.7 miles, pull into the Biscuit Brook parking area on the left.

This demanding and fascinating scenic tour takes you through the upper-elevation backcountry of the Big Indian Wilderness Area in the southern Catskills. You will ride at an average elevation of 2,000 feet, first along a fairly flat section of road adjacent to the West Branch of the Neversink, then onto a higher-elevation loop in the Willowemoc Wild Forest. The section of this tour that follows West Branch Road between the Biscuit Brook Trailhead parking area and the Blue Hill Road bridge, is our favorite bike ride in the Catskills.

If you have any romantic notions about biking for brookies, here's the place to try it; you will pass two public fishing access points on both the Fir and Willowemoc creeks. Bikers wishing to camp out can do so in the beautiful primitive sites on Flugertown Road next to the creek, located

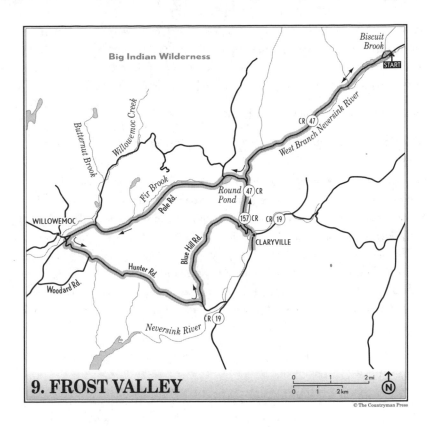

Big Indian Wilderness

9. FROST VALLEY

© The Countryman Press

roughly halfway through the tour. There's a lean-to on Long Pond in the southern Willowemoc Wild Forest that mountain bikers looking for an out-of-the-way campsite can reach with some effort. You can even book a room at the YMCA camp in Frost Valley (check dates and seasons), or in any of the several mountain houses and inns on Slide Mountain Road that you'll pass en route to the trailhead parking area. However you approach this tour, you will come away having experienced the true heart of the heart of the wild, unspoiled Catskill Mountains.

0.00 From the Biscuit Brook Trailhead parking area, go left (west) on West Branch Road (a.k.a. Frost Valley Road, CR 47). Pass Frost Valley's maple sugarhouse on the right.

1.40 Pass the Frost Valley YMCA camp, a large complex of beautifully built conference and program buildings on both sides of the road.

Soon you will draw close to the Neversink's West Branch, the blue-green, shallow moun-tain river that has been carving its way through this high valley from the western slopes of Slide Mountain for 15 thousand years or so. Deep blue shimmering hemlock forests shade the creek. The hills of the Peekamoose Wild Forest rise to the south.

6.80 Turn right onto Round Pond Road and ascend.

7.50 Bear left. Round Pond (private) is to your left. Leave Bear Road to your right.

Riders wishing to ride only the loop section of this tour can begin at the Black Bear Trailhead parking area, 0.2 mile ahead on Bear Road. The Black Bear Trailhead is also a good choice for mountain bikers who want to ride in to Long Pond lean-to, using (steep) Basily Road and the level, red-blazed Long Pond–Beaverkill Ridge Trail (Flugertown Road trailheads can also be used).

Round Pond Road becomes Pole Road now as you cross into Sullivan County. Many early roads in the Catskills were surfaced with planks or poles to prevent rutting and mir-ing, and such surfaces could bear heavy wagonloads of freight. Local farmers were paid by their respective towns to maintain them.

11.00 Pass the Fir Brook fishing access parking area on the right. Here is the realm of the wild brook trout.

11.20 Pass Flugertown/Brown's Road to the right. The Willowemoc primitive camping sites (free) are located on Flugertown Road, 1 mile to the north.

12.30 Turn left on Cooley/Parksville Road and go a few hundred feet to Hunter Road. Bear left on Hunter Road. This is a cruelly steep climb.

Note: If you need supplies or a telephone, there's a private campsite with a small general store in Willowemoc, just to the west on Willowemoc Road.

13.30 Pass Woodard Road on your right as Hunter Road levels out. Following is a steep, short descent to a swampy area above Conklin Brook.

Views open up to the west and south from high open fields. There are several dense Norway spruce plantations in the vicinity. The long, high ridge to the south is the Shawangunk Ridge.

15.50 The road descends steeply and becomes a seasonal-use road (dirt).

16.50 Turn left onto Blue Hill Road and climb across the southerly slopes of Blue Hill, heading north now.

As you top out along the northern slopes, there are fascinating views of the Catskill High Peaks area, including Table, Peekamoose, and Slide mountains in the Slide Mountain Wilderness Area.

19.50 Head downhill very steeply now on a seasonal-use highway (dirt).

20.10 Arrive at CR 157 (West Branch Road, Frost Valley Road). You will turn left here.

To your right, across the bridge, the road heads to Claryville. There's a small general store in Claryville, requiring a 0.6-mile detour from your present position. (To reach it, turn right and go 0.2 mile to CR 19, then left on CR 19 for 0.4 mile).

Head north on CR 157 to the point where it becomes CR 42 at the intersection with Round Pond Road. Retrace your steps from here back through Frost Valley to the Biscuit Brook Trailhead parking area.

The Frost Valley YMCA has many membership programs that are open to the public, including hiking and wildlife observation, rifle, muzzleloader, and bow hunting, trout fishing, and upland game hunting. They have a system of marked cross-country ski trails as well. The Y owns 6,000 acres of land around the West and East Branch of the Neversink, which is in turn surrounded by over 100,000 acres of Catskill forest preserve, wild forest, and wilderness areas. Inquire with the Director of Natural Resources, Frost Valley YMCA, 2000 Frost Valley Road, Claryville, NY 12725. The telephone number is 845-985-2291, and the web site is www.frostvalley.org.

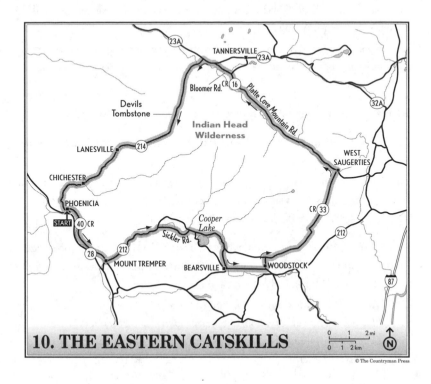

10. THE EASTERN CATSKILLS

© The Countryman Press

One More Notch: The Eastern Catskills

DISTANCE: 42.6 miles

CUMULATIVE ELEVATION GAIN: 3400 feet

TERRAIN: Very hilly

DIFFICULTY: Strenuous

RECOMMENDED BICYCLE: Mountain, hybrid, road (no dirt)

DIRECTIONS

Phoenicia is 23 miles west of Kingston Exit 19 off the New York State Thruway (I-87). Turn right off NY 28 into the village and park on NY 214, immediately off Main Street in the town parking lot, or use street parking.

Here's an ambitious day ride with lots of hills and rivers, including a historic mountain pass or two. (It's a long day trip for a mountain bike.) The ride will introduce you to the eastern Catskill Mountain villages of Tannersville, Phoenicia, and Woodstock, and give you a good look at the big wilderness areas of the Catskills' high, dissected plateau and the Catskill Escarpment. You begin south of the scarp on the Esopus floodplain, where the hills taper off into the flatlands and then climb through it at Platte Clove. For the average rider this route may be on the long and strenuous side, but there are plenty of services along the way. You can travel light, have lunch on the road, and deal easily with bike-related needs or repairs in the two bike shops you'll pass.

First, an explanation. We wanted to create a tour in the Phoenicia area and tried out several ideas for interesting circular routes before deciding on this one. We looked at the balloon tour to Mount Tremper,

Bearsville, Lake Hill, Willow, and back to Phoenicia. We also researched what looked like a very interesting ride through Silver Hollow that connects Willow to Edgewood. Our test ride through this remote mountain pass proved to us that the Silver Hollow Road (still a town road), although not entirely impassable, would prove an annoying and hazardous ordeal—for the road is washed out, rocky, and nearly reclaimed by nature after 80 years of disuse. There is no doubt that it can be done, but not comfortably, safely, or even easily, especially in all but the heaviest cycling shoes. And you'd have to portage your bike for over 1 mile on sharp, moss-laden rocks, over blowdowns, through mud, and so on to make the connection with NY 214. Because we realized that some riders would see that route on the map (especially county maps, where it looks passable), we figured it would be wise to issue fair warning. The following route is a real ride in the mountains.

0.00 From the municipal lot in Phoenicia, pull out of town on CR 40, heading southeast.

This is a lined road that's fairly well traveled by skilled road cyclists. The shoulder is variable, but mostly poor. Motorists are not particularly bike-savvy. On the outskirts of town, you will ride beside the Esopus Creek, a very popular trout stream in the Charmed Circle class of rivers (that group of fabled trout rivers lying between Pennsylvania's Letort and the famous Beaverkill in New York). There are several access areas where you can pull over for a look. The river is popular with tubers, so you may see a few of them, drifting past the fisherman. Pass the Phoenicia–Mount Tremper Trail to the Mount Tremper fire tower on your left.

3.75 At Mount Tremper Corners, turn left onto NY 212. (We considered using CR 40 into Bearsville but decided that it is too bike-unfriendly and fast).

There was a Revolutionary War stockade here, and later, the Catskills' first railroad hotel, where Oscar Wilde delivered his aesthetic lectures. You've got a steady climb ahead of you now.

7.20 The road flattens out through Willow (no services).

To the north lie the lesser peaks of the Indian Head Wilderness Area and the Mount Tremper Wild Forest. You're riding along next to the Beaver Kill (not to be confused with the infamous Beaverkill).

7.35 Bear right onto Sickler Road to cut off a section of the busier NY 212.

9.00 Rejoin NY 212 and turn right.

9.60 Pass Cooper Lake and continue along NY 212.
This is the city of Kingston's water supply. You can turn right here to circle this incredibly scenic reservoir (dirt), rejoining this route at the intersection of NY 212 and CR 45. Use Ride 11 for reference. Note that there is some dirt involved in using this option.

10.60 Pass Church Road on the left. If you want to add a hill climb (600 vertical feet) through Meads, turn left here (for details, see Ride 11). Descend into Bearsville.

12.40 Turn left on NY 212 and head into Woodstock.

14.20 Enter Woodstock.

There are plenty of places to eat. We suggest Catskill Mountain Pizza on Tinker Street because you can eat at one of the outdoor tables and watch your bike. The food's fantastic, too, and reasonably priced.

14.20 At the Village Green, turn left onto Rock City Road, pass the venerable Family of Woodstock (if you need an extra sweater you can get one here), Andy Lee Field, and the Woodstock Community Center. Traffic is mellow (if you will).

14.90 Turn right onto Glasco Turnpike (CR 33).

16.60 Turn left off Glasco Turnpike and continue on CR 33 (West Saugerties Road).
Now you have a long, level ride with mountain scenery. The large mountain to your left is Overlook, and the ridge extending to the north is Plattekill. Traffic is relatively relaxed through here, and there are long straightaways with good sight distance.

21.20 Turn left onto Platte Clove Mountain Road. Be careful, this is a totally blind turn to the left. Granny your way up through Platte Clove for about 3 miles and 1,400 feet, vertical (for details, see Ride 3), and flatten out on top.
You're in the woods now! Continue along, enjoying the spectacular scenery of the Indian Head Wilderness Area to your left. The road becomes CR 16 and heads into Tannersville. You can jog through Tannersville (see Ride 3), or continue straight ahead to NY 23A. But if you want food or need to visit Phil Theo's bike shop (Philthy O's), you'll have to go into vibrantly colorful Tannersville (well worth a visit).

28.80 Bear left on Bloomer Road.

29.80 Bear left on NY 23A. This is a busy state road, but the shoulders are good and you get off it shortly.

30.50 Turn left on NY 214.

This is a nice, straight road, but traffic can be fast. That big mountain straight ahead is Hunter, the Catskills' second highest peak. To the right you can see the Hunter Mountain Ski Area.

32.20 Just beyond a state land historical plaque, pass a piped spring on your right.

Now you're heading into Stony Clove, the mountain pass that was used by the first railroads that came to the great Catskill mountain houses. The clove forms a deep V here, called Stony Clove Notch. This is where the western flanks of Plateau Mountain meet the eastern slopes of Hunter Mountain.

33.40 Pass Notch Lake in the heart of the Notch.

There's a day-use area and picnic tables on the right. The Devil's Path trunk trail passes through here on its way to Hunter and West Kill mountains.

33.70 Pass the Devil's Tombstone state campground and public use area (telephone).

37.60 Go through Lanesville.

This town seems to deserve the name Logging Capital of the World. There are large piles of timber and firewood, and lots of logging equipment. Come downhill through pretty Chichester (no services), following along next to Chichester Brook, and continue downhill, taking care through a few blind curves. There is no shun route; the peripheral terrain is too steep.

42.60 Arrive in the piscatorial town of Phoenicia.

Enjoy yourself with a well-earned pizza and beer at the Sportsman's, or just a pizza at Brio's. (The two are jointly owned, but only the Sportsman's serves beer. Both have quaint, sidewalk tables.) To give you an idea of what kind of a town Phoenicia is, after dinner one night we watched a bear sucking spaghetti out of Brio's dumpster in the back parking lot. Beyond, at high water we could hear the Esopus Creek's rapids.

11

Three Days of Peace and Music: Woodstock

DISTANCE: 13.2 miles

CUMULATIVE ELEVATION GAIN: 1800 feet

TERRAIN: Hilly

DIFFICULTY: Strenuous

RECOMMENDED BICYCLE: Mountain, hybrid, road

DIRECTIONS

From Saugerties, Exit 20 of the New York State Thruway (I-87), drive west on NY 212, 8.7 miles to Woodstock. As you come into town, NY 212 becomes Tinker Street. In the center of the village, watch for Rock City Road on the right, just before the Village Green. Turn right and go a short distance to Andy Lee Field and the Woodstock Community Center parking area (just past the Woodstock Artist's Cemetery).

Although the *real* Woodstock Festival took place at Yasgur's Farm in Bethel, New York, this ride takes place in the *real* Woodstock, New York, where the festival should have been. And what's so real about Woodstock, anyway? Real big hills. But don't let that deter you from experiencing the self-described, hippest small town in America. This town is so cool it has its own community bicycle (finding it is the problem). If you can find it, you can just grab it anytime you want to do an errand. It has a sign hung from the top tube that says COMMUNITY BICYCLE, PLEASE RETURN AFTER USE.

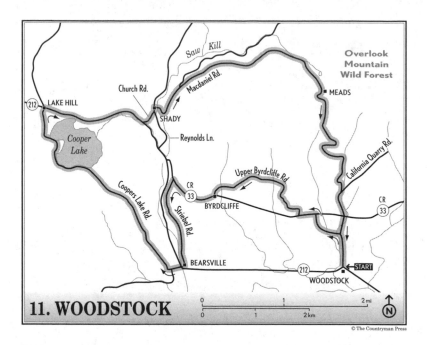

11. WOODSTOCK

© The Countryman Press

0.00 Start the tour from Andy Lee Field, just north of the Village Green, next to the Woodstock Community Center on Rock City Road. Turn right out of Andy Lee Field parking area.

0.20 Turn left onto Lower Byrdcliffe Road at Parnassus Square. This is a lined road through a pretty section of town. Traffic is light.

0.60 Turn left onto Glasco Turnpike, CR 33.

This was a turnpike 150 years ago. After the Catskills had been stripped of their hemlocks by the mid- to late 1800s, other industries sprang up to strip the area of the hardwoods that took their place, namely, furniture and glass-making. (Glasco is a contraction of Glass Company.)

0.78 Turn right onto Upper Byrdcliffe Road. Climb through beautiful oak and pine woods. There are a few houses.

1.60 Enter the area that formed the heart of the original Byrdcliffe Art Colony.

You'll see brown, rustic lodges that are still rented to fine artists and writers, as well as the Byrdcliffe Theater, where you can take a guide map for the Byrdcliffe walking tour.

Continue on the road, as some views of the Catskills open up in the west.

2.10 Pass the legendary Byrdcliffe Barn, where dances and theatrical events are regularly held.

2.20 Turn right onto Glasco Turnpike and climb easily.

2.80 Turn left onto Striebel Road. To the right beyond the guardrail, the terrain pitches down sharply to the Saw Kill Valley. Enjoy a nice long descent.

3.90 Turn right onto NY 212 in Bearsville.

The town is named for Christian Baehr who had a store here in 1839. Across the road is the beloved Bearsville Theater and two charming restaurants, the Big Bear and the Little Bear, the latter poised magically above the Saw Kill.

Cross the Saw Kill and remain on NY 212.

4.00 Turn right onto Coopers Lake Road and climb.

The area speed limit is 30 mph, but some of the citizenry may be navigating celestially, so drive defensively. This is one of the prettiest back roads in the Catskills. Climb steadily now.

5.20 The road turns to dirt. The houses are magnificent and charming.

5.60 As you approach Cooper Lake, dense forests appear.

These pines form the buffer zone around the lake, the city of Kingston's water supply. The scenery is spectacular now as you ride along the lake's edge in view of the Indian Head Wilderness Area to the north.

6.00 Views of Overlook Mountain appear to the right.

Against the northern sky, from east to west, are Indian Head, Twin, and Plateau mountains. This area is the site of one of the many anti-rent skirmishes in the Catskills, part of the larger movement known as the Anti-Rent Wars. Tenant farmers, already struggling to grow crops in the relatively poor mountain soils, rebelled against the Livingston patentees who demanded increasing rents. The farmers dressed up as Native Americans so as not to be recognizable and rioted. After many years and the unintentional killing of a sheriff's deputy, the patents were broken up by an act of the New York legislature, the farmers retained their lands, and many continued to farm the area. There is substantial evidence that the real Johnny Appleseed lived up in the Mink Hollow area.

The Indian Head Wilderness Area from the northern realms of Meads Mountain

6.80 Turn right off of Coopers Lake Road onto NY 212. Stay right and keep to the shoulder. There's a fog line, centerline, and guardrail. The shoulder improves somewhat. The excellent lake scenery continues for a short distance.

6.80 Watch carefully now, and turn left onto Church Road. Use caution when crossing NY 212. Climb past the Methodist Church of Shady.

8.20 Turn left at the corner of Church Road and Reynolds Lane.

8.25 Turn right onto Macdaniel Road (a.k.a. Macdaniels Mountain Road) and cross the Saw Kill. A long climb follows.

Views of the Devil's Path mountains open up to the north. The mountain beyond Indian Head Farm is Indian Head Mountain. This is a long, slow ascent.

10.80 Top out in Meads, at the site of the Karma Triyana Dharmachakra Tibetan Buddhist Monastery.

There's a gift shop inside. The monks welcome visitors. Meditation and prayer workshops are offered to the public and are well worth the time if you're at all curious about Tibetan life and culture. Sometimes the sessions are free, but more involved instruction is fee-based. To join in meditation, you need to have the ability to sit still quietly for a very long time. Across from the monastery is the Overlook Mountain Trailhead parking area. A little north of this lot is an open field called Magic Meadow, the sacred ground of the Woodstock Rainbow Tribe (don't worry, you're already a member). This area has been the site of many strange events and is said to be a vortex zone. Below the monastery and dwarfed by it lies the little brown church of Christ on the Mount, pulpit of Father William Francis, the legendary hippie priest.

You will agree that Meads is indeed a magical spot, where considerable forces emit from the earth, because you are about to encounter one of these considerable forces now: gravity. Prepare for a long, steep descent. Tighten up your gear, adjust your helmet properly, and be careful—the road is winding and steep. You can see Sky Top in Mohonk from the upper reaches of Meads, as well as other points in the northern Shawangunks. Keep your eyes on the road, though, and take the plunge, feathering your breaks.

12.50 Pass California Quarry Road.

This was the site of an early bluestone quarry, as well as an area where extensive archaeological work has been undertaken in an early Native American hunting camp, circa B.C. 2000 to A.D. 750.

12.80 Bottom out at Glasco Four Corners, and slowly go through the intersection, crossing NY 212 onto Rock City Road.

Rock in this context is in reference to California Quarry, not the festival.

13.20 Turn left into Andy Lee Field.

Enjoy a look around town! You'll soon discover that Woodstock has New York prices. We like having coffee at Bread Alone on Tinker Street (where everybody who's anybody likes to be seen), but we like to eat at Maria's Bizarre (also try Heaven). Our favorite bistro is Catskill Mountain Pizza, on NY 212 (a.k.a. Mill Hill Road), just before you get to the Village Green coming from the east. For bike rentals, sales, and repair, don't forget to visit Billy Denter at Overlook Mountain Bikes (see Appendix).

12

A Few Red Cents: Denning

DISTANCE: 17 miles out-and-back; 11.2-mile loop

CUMULATIVE ELEVATION GAIN: 500 feet; 1300 feet

TERRAIN: Rolling; Hilly

DIFFICULTY: Easy; Moderate

RECOMMENDED BICYCLE: Mountain, hybrid, road

DIRECTIONS

From the intersection of NY 28 and CR 42 in Big Indian, bear left (south) on CR 42 (a.k.a. Slide Mountain Road). At 7.5 miles, pass the Giant Ledge parking area, and farther on, Winnisook Lake. Pass the Frost Valley YMCA at 14 miles. At 20 miles, turn right on CR 19 in Claryville. Park at the little tannery turnout on the right at 0.3 mile.

Here's a beautiful ride alongside the Neversink River that you can take as an out-and-back tour or with a high, scenic return loop across Red Hill. The first section of the ride begins in Claryville and ends at the Phoenicia East Branch Trailhead in the Slide Mountain Wilderness Area. These are the headwaters of the Neversink's East Branch, one of the highest, most remote river valleys in the Catskills. While most of the road is surrounded by the private lands of the Frost Valley YMCA, there's an island of state land on the river, partway through the tour, where you can picnic and fish; and there's the wilderness area at the turnaround point. However you chose to handle this tour, you'll be happy that you experienced this unusually appealing area of the Catskills.

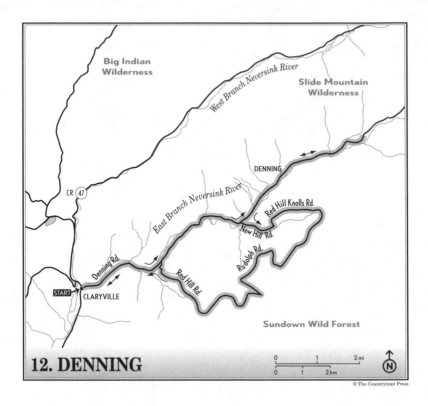

12. DENNING

© The Countryman Press

0.00 From the tannery parking area, bear left and go along CR 19 (Denning Road) back through Claryville, a diffuse little settlement with a New England character, lying at the confluence of the Neversink's East and West Branch. You'll be following the East Branch.

0.90 Go through the village where there's a post office and the Claryville Country Store. A bit beyond these you will pass the Claryville Town Hall (where there's also room to park if the tannery lot is full). At the corner of Wildcat Mountain Road, continue straight on Denning Road. You'll notice yellow state trail markers here and there, indicating that this road leads to the Phoenicia–East Branch Trailhead, which is yellow-blazed. You'll cross the Neversink several times ahead.

2.60 Pass Red Hill Road on the right. Denning Road ascends slightly as it travels alongside the river.

4.90 Pass New Hill Road on the right. (This is the point at which you will turn left on your return to circle Red Hill.)

6.20 Pass the YMCA's Education Camp. YMCA postings appear.

You will see a sign detailing the YMCA's reforestation and selective thinning efforts, explaining how selective cuts are beneficial to forests. (The tendency of most people is to suspect that any logging is a bad thing.) It is true the logging that the Y is conducting here contrasts sharply with the forest preserve's hands-off, constitutionally created forever wild policy. But this is a working forest on private lands, and management policies are different. The Y takes great pride in the condition and health of their forests, a fact that can be seen in the resource as you travel through it.

Forests that are managed selectively are often healthier, grow faster, and are less prone to disease than those left to normal succession. Managers allow the trees that are best suited for the site to attain dominance. Thus, managed forests, such as the pine and spruce plantations you see in the Catskills, are often more aesthetically pleasing than wild forests.

7.00 Pass a state land public use area next to the creek. You can pull over and sit next to the water here.

7.10 Pass the YMCA's Strauss Center on the right.

8.50 Arrive at the Denning Trailhead, parking area, and hiker's kiosk.

Situated in an open field, this is a pretty spot where the deer often come to feed. One time we rolled apples that had fallen from a nearby tree to a group of deer. The deer ran after them as if it was some kind of a very fun game.

If you want, you can camp legally inside the wilderness area here if you observe the forest preserve's rules: no camping within 150 feet of a trail or water source. You can't ride your bike here, however, because it's wilderness, but you can walk your bike far enough into the woods to find a suitable campsite. The first part of the trail is a dirt road.

In our humble opinions, the area around the confluence of the East Branch and Deer Shanty Brook is one of the most alluring and captivating in the Catskills. For many years this area was the most popular staging ground for climbers heading to Slide Mountain (the Catskills' highest peak), as well as nearby Peekamoose and Table. There is also a popular bushwhack route from the confluence to the col between Slide and Cornell mountains.

The confluence was intensively used and consciously—even recklessly—abused; hikers camped on the stream's edge, creating fire rings and other impacts (such as the rampant cutting of live trees), and wore the forest floor down to mineral soil. In the mid-'70s, there were about a hundred of these little campsites. The state's removal of the lean-to, along with NO CAMPING postings and reclamation efforts, has helped to return this beautiful spot to its natural state.

The town of Denning is named for William Denning, who purchased most of his 24 thousand acres from a Philadelphia land grant corporation that failed to pay its taxes. The price was one cent per acre in 1841.

Turn around and head back the way you came, to mile 4.9 at New Hill Road. Reset to zero.

The high, golden potato fields of Red Hill, cultivated from 1850, are barren today, leaving open, rounded hills. In the forest's edge, modest seasonal residences have sprung up. A buffer zone of protected forest land is owned by the YMCA, and extensive state lands all but surround the little inholding of Red Hill with its heirloom fire tower: Sundown Wild Forest, the Big Indian Wilderness, and the Slide Mountain Wilderness. This little-known area in the southwestern Catskills is big on scenery, however—a fact verified by the long-lasting reign of the Red Hill fire tower, built in 1920 at 2,980 feet to become the last staffed tower (along with Hunter mountain's) in the Catskills. But you don't have to climb the tower (the trail can't be biked) to take advantage of the huge panoramic views from the surrounding hills. According to the DEC, this view includes "the largest area of productive forest land (outside the Catskill Forest Preserve) in the region."

0.00 Ascend New Hill Road.

0.70 Turn left on Red Hill Knolls Road (a.k.a. Red Hill Road). This is high, pretty country. The surface is pavement. There are no lines or shoulders. The lands here belong to the YMCA.

1.80 Pass Kawliga Road on the left. The road flattens a little.

2.20 Pass Porcupine Road and begin a descent.

3.30 Climbing again, you will have views to the south of the Rondout Reservoir.

4.00 Turn right at the intersection onto Red Hill Road. The road's quality diminishes.

4.30 Turn left onto Rudolph Road, a delightful dirt one laner.

5.40 Intersect Dinch Road at Barefoot Corner. Turn left and descend on a gravel surface. The red soil here that gives the area its name is glacial silt.

6.00 Turn right on Red Hill Road and follow it back to Denning Road.

8.70 Turn left on Denning Road. Retrace your route to the parking area.

11.20 Arrive at the tannery parking area.

13

The Holy Grail: Peekamoose Clove to Vernooy Kill Falls

DISTANCE: 35 miles

CUMULATIVE ELEVATION GAIN: 4750 feet

TERRAIN: Very hilly

DIFFICULTY: Strenuous

RECOMMENDED BICYCLE: Mountain, hybrid

DIRECTIONS

The ride begins in West Shokan, which lies at the extreme western end of the Ashokan Reservoir. From Boiceville, turn south off NY 28 onto NY 28A. (You will immediately cross the Esopus Creek.) At 3 miles turn right onto CR 42 (Peekamoose Road) at West Shokan, and within 200 feet take the first left onto Lang Street. Turn right into Davis Park. (There is more parking on the town garage side of the park.) There are phones and rest rooms here. For last-minute needs, the American General Store is 0.2 mile farther along NY 28A in West Shokan.

This spellbinding, unforgettable ride will introduce you to the interior Catskill Forest Preserve, where you will ride next to some of the cleanest rivers in the country and witness the uncommonly savage terrain of several wild forests and a larger expanse of forever wild lands—the Slide Mountain Wilderness. The loop is suitable as a day ride if you begin early, but it might be most appreciated as an overnight bikepacking experience. Here is a good chance to shake down for extended touring over varied terrain.

Of the major cloves in the Catskills, the easterly Kaaterskill Clove and Platte Clove are the most popular. Compared to these, not many

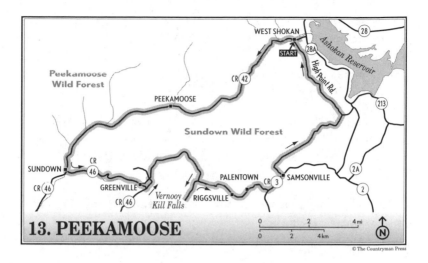

people venture into Peekamoose Clove (a.k.a. Peekamoose Gorge) to the southwest. It is somewhat off the beaten track for summer visitors and weekend tourists; its main road brings you through an isolated back-country where there are few, if any, amenities besides the wilderness. (Come well equipped.) It is a land of waterfalls; headwater creeks; crumbling, moss-clad talus slopes; twisted blowdowns; and remote trailheads to the Catskills' highest mountains.

If all of this has you thinking hills, you're on the right track. One of the features of the Catskill landscape that has sustained the privacy of its trails and peaks is the very sudden elevation gain from sea level. This daunting rise quickly weeds out casual visitors, assuring the solitude of the realm for those who come prepared to suffer a little. Forest management people call this self-limiting terrain because the steepness tends to limit overuse by weeding out casual visitors. The roads, of course, are a little different. You will see weekend warriors car-camped at the Sundown primitive area (Morrell Field) and sometimes a fast-moving group of touring motorcyclists passing through. Less often, but increasingly present, are cyclists, heading to the Holy Grail for a substantial workout. Once off the road in the upper elevations of Sundown Wild Forest, you will see few, if any, people as you work your way over remote dirt roads to the even less used Vernooy Kill Falls area.

Carry enough water for the entire ride or use a quality filter when drinking from natural sources. Ride the loop later in the season if you are adverse to bugs—there is a good deal of standing water in Sundown Forest, and black flies can be an issue in the Catskills during springtime. Also, if you plan to do this tour in a single day, carry road lights.

0.00 Exit Davis Park and turn left (west) onto CR 42 (Peekamoose Road). There is a centerline and a fog line but less than a 1-foot wide paved shoulder. Traffic is slow-moving and sparse. The scenery is of mountains and improves with more mountains as you cross Maltby Hollow Brook.

0.40 Note High Point Mountain Road on the left—it is the road you will return on. Begin climbing gradually.

2.75 Pass South Hollow Road on the left.

In dire circumstances, you can camp in a primitive setting at the end of this road, but it re-quires a four-wheel drive or other high-ground-clearance vehicle because there is a rocky road and a substantial stream crossing (dry in summer) leading to the site. Peekamoose Road steepens. State land appears on the left.

3.90 Pass the Kanape Brook Trailhead parking area on the right. There's a chemical toilet here. This is the trailhead to Ashokan High Point. Now the road climbs in earnest, entering the more remote woods where the Sundown Wild Forest and the Slide Mountain Wilderness Area abut one another. The road is better now—double-lined all the way with an improved shoulder. Granny your way up into the clove. Sharp ridges rise all around.

5.00 The road levels, then drifts downhill.

Steep ridges rise to the north and south. This is the headwater terrain of the Rondout Creek, which materializes slowly on the left, increasing in volume as it descends. Slide talus appears and the scenery becomes alpine and otherworldly.

6.00 Pass heartbreakingly beautiful Peekamoose Lake (private) and a private estate gatehouse on your right. Descend, passing a waterfall on the right (also private but there's a better one ahead on state land).

Now you are in the interior clove. The scenery is dramatic. You'll see raptors—possibly ea-gles. Road lines disappear, shoulders are gravel; speed limit is 30 mph and seldom heeded by the few cars in this section—but those that come are sightseeing, not necessarily watching the road! Dirt pull-offs are fishing access sites. The Rondout is native brook trout water.

8.40 Double lines pick up again. The road follows next to the creek.

8.80 Pass a waterfall on your right (public). Note that the falls emanates from a subterranean source. This is Buttermilk Falls. You can pull off and rest here, of course, but a better choice lies just ahead.

10.00 The Peekamoose Mountain Trailhead appears on the right. Accordingly, there are trail signs posted here.

This trail (also the Long Path, a trail that goes from the George Washington Bridge to the Helderbergs) penetrates the Slide Mountain Wilderness Area, crossing Peekamoose Mountain (3,843 feet) and Table (3,847 feet) on its way to Slide Mountain (4,190 feet), the Catskills' highest peak.

This part is important: Just before you reach this trailhead parking area, back up the road a few hundred feet on the south side, a footpath leads down to a secret swimming spot—the legendary Blue Hole. You can wheel your bike down the trail (it's short). If you don't visit this remarkably clear pool on the Rondout, you're missing the Holy Grail.

10.20 The Sundown Wild Forest/ Peekamoose Valley Morrell Field parking area is on the right.

This is the small residential area known as Bull Run. The campsite is extensive and continues for another mile to the lower field. Camping is free and on the creek. Permits are required for motorized campers. The phone numbers of supervising rangers are listed at a kiosk by the upper field, but cell phones don't work here. Those with questions or in need of permits must contact the DEC Region 3 office ahead of time. A very rugged foot trail departs for the Vernooy Kill Falls area (the Long Path) on the left (south) side of the road just opposite the upper field parking area.

Continue down the road, freewheeling through Bull Run.

On your left, not too far west of the camping area, is a small store, open during the camping season.

13.00 Arrive at Sundown, a three-way intersection, and bear left (south) onto CR 46 (Sundown-Greenville Road), leaving the United Methodist Church to your right. Take care not to get on White House Road. There is a vague centerline and no shoulders. Ascend steeply.

16.50 Pass Cross Road on the left and ascend.

16.90 Reach the corner of Dymond Road and CR 46. There is a pull-off on the right where it is suitable to park a car. Turn left onto Dymond Road. Immediately on the right you will see a trailhead that leads to Vernooy Kill Falls and Cherrytown Road. Don't follow this trail. Instead, continue straight ahead, traveling northeast on Dymond Road.

17.40 At the intersection of Cross and Dymond Roads, bear right onto Spencer Road (unmarked), which departs to the right. This is actually a town road. Old trail signs may still be seen here. The road is dirt and can be very muddy. It is also extremely rocky. The combination of the two will make for rough going, but persevere—things will improve dramatically, ahead.

18.50 Continue straight where a dirt road departs to the right. Blue trail markers will appear (Long Path).

18.60 Pass a small house (hunting camp) on the left.

19.30 Cross a little bridge over the Vernooy Kill. Just across the bridge on the other side of the creek is an ideal place to camp. (The GPS coordinates are N41 degrees, 53", 880'/W074 degrees, 22", 548', and the elevation is 2,000 feet.) Although this is an excellent place to camp, Vernooy Kill Falls is far better and lies ahead.

20.00 At this point, the Long Path departs to the right for Vernooy Kill Falls. (For information on this trail, see the AMC's *Catskill Mountain Guide*.) Don't take it. Instead, continue straight ahead, bearing southwest. The road improves dramatically. Thick woods is the norm, including hemlock stands, mountain laurel, sugar maple, and beech trees.

21.30 Arrive at a three-way intersection. (GPS coordinates are N41 degrees, 53", 062'/W074 degrees, 21", 636', and the elevation is 1,950 feet.) Camping is permitted here in a highly impacted site, but this area is accessible from Trail's End Road and therefore is not secluded. Your route continues straight ahead on Trail's End Road, but the out-and-back trail to Vernooy Kill Falls goes off to the right (south) around a barrier gate. Turn right and proceed. You can ride 95 percent of this trail, walking around a couple of rocky areas.

22.50 Arrive at Vernooy Kill Falls. When you're prepared to leave, backtrack to the three-way intersection (mile 21.3).

Legal campsites abound here, but the best one is positioned on a low hill to the left, just to the right of the trail to Upper Cherrytown Road. There's a privy. The falls runs in a succes-

sion of rapids. An unmarked trail to the right of the bridge follows upstream to many pri-
vate spots. Another foot trail leaves from the south side of the bridge and heads down-
stream. There are several trail signs here to keep you oriented.

Just downstream of the bridge on the left-hand side of the river, you will see the stone
remains of a gristmill. It was at this site in the early 1700s that Cornelius Vernooy built the
first gristmill in the town of Wawarsing. It is believed that he brought the components for a
gristmill with him from Holland. Local farming had grown to a point where a production
mill was needed. Without sophisticated milling equipment, it was impossible for individ-
ual farmers to produce enough grist by hand to provide for their families, and even then it
was a coarse product suitable only for meal. Vernooy's mill enabled the creation of bread
flour on a large scale, and farmers from 50 miles around brought their wagons, bearing a
season's worth of grain, to this site for milling. Later, in 1755, when more industrial-weight
milling equipment was developed, a mill appeared on the much larger Rondout Creek.

23.70 Continue on Trail's End Road, which goes downhill and turns to pavement. The road passes a few camps and odd dwellings.

25.40 Merge into Sundown Road, bearing left.

25.70 Bear left onto Palentown Road (also referenced as Upper Cherrytown
Road).

26.50 Bear right onto Rocky Mountain (a.k.a. Rocky) Road.

This is a somewhat roundabout way to shun a short section of the busier CR 3, or
Samsonville Road. If you'd rather not go the extra distance, you can simply turn right at
the corner of Rocky Mountain and Palentown Roads and turn left on Samsonville Road.

26.90 Pass Palentown cemetery. Good views of Ashokan High Point are en-
joyed here.

27.10 Turn left on CR 3, Samsonville Road. Be more careful now. This is a country road, but traffic is faster and shoulders are less than ideal.

28.00 Turn left onto quiet Upper Samsonville Road. Ascend.

What follows for the remainder of the trip involves attractive, rural residential areas with
views of the surrounding mountains and the Ashokan Reservoir to the east (on your
right) as you travel north into the Peekamoose Valley.

28.50 Bear right at Haver Road, remaining on Upper Samsonville Road.
Descend.

23.70 At CR 3, Samsonville Road, go left.

32.30 Turn left onto High Point Mountain Road (a.k.a. High Point Road). Begin a descent.

35.00 Go straight (bearing left) where the road curves into West Shokan Heights Road, remaining on High Point Road. Descend!

36.20 Back in West Shokan! Bear right onto CR 42, Peekamoose Road.

36.70 Arrive at Davis Park. You've found the grail and are thereby admitted to paradise.

14

By a Dam Site: The Ashokan Reservoir

DISTANCE: 7 miles

CUMULATIVE ELEVATION GAIN: 450 feet

TERRAIN: Gently rolling to flat

DIFFICULTY: Easy

RECOMMENDED BICYCLE: Mountain, hybrid, road

DIRECTIONS

From Kingston Exit 19 of the New York State Thruway, set to zero and travel west on NY 28 toward Phoenicia. At 1 mile, pass Kenco, the Work and Play Outfitter (take a look). At 12 miles, turn left onto Reservoir Road at Winchells Corners and enter the buffer zone of the Ashokan Reservoir. Cross the dividing weir. Views of the Catskills are phenomenal from here. At 13.8 miles, turn left onto Monument Road (the dike to your left is part of the route you'll soon be traveling). Go down the hill and bear left onto NY 28A, and at 15.3 miles, turn left into the Frying Pan. The pan is formed by Leonard Hill Circle, where you'll park; the Middle Dike forms the handle where you'll ride. There's an information kiosk with maps located here.

The second you leave the Frying Pan to cross the Ashokan's Middle Dike, you will agree that this amazing ride is among the most scenic bike tours anywhere. You will be introduced to some of the more pleasant roads around the reservoir as well, framed by the extensive, upper-elevation backdrop of the Slide Mountain Wilderness Area—the heart of the Catskill High Peaks. These are the best views of the Catskill mountains you can get without actually climbing them!

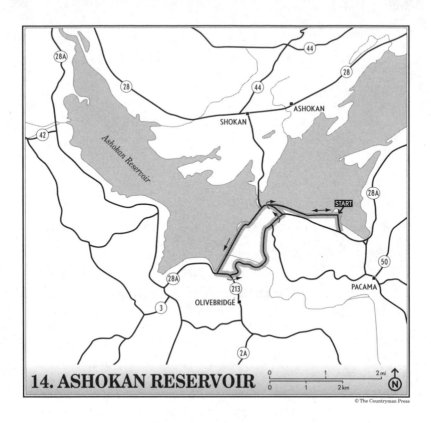

14. ASHOKAN RESERVOIR

© The Countryman Press

The ride is short, but you will find yourself lingering along the dikes, near the main dam, and around the aerator, so allow an hour or more. While this tour is recommended to intermediate riders because of the two well-traveled roads that are used, the first 1.3 miles is closed to motor vehicle traffic. It is used regularly by skaters, strollers, bicyclists with tag-a-longs, tiny children on trainers, and artists with their easels and palettes set up facing the surrounding wilderness areas. This is a very popular spot with locals who appear for regular workouts and saunters, but it is never too busy to enjoy.

There is no practical loop around the reservoir itself without using NY 28—a dangerous, heavily used highway that is best avoided, and there is no opportunity to enter the beautiful, boreal forests of the buffer zone on a bike, or on foot, without a permit. Also, since the Cat-skill Reservoir system provides New York City with water, security has been heightened since 9/11, and fines may be levied upon those who cross the well-marked boundaries around the impoundment. Department of Environmental Protection (DEP) police heavily patrol the area.

In spite of the restrictions, the scenic wonder of the place is overwhelming, and for a region with few natural lakes, the reservoirs provide an idea of what the post-glacial lake that existed here some 17 thousand years ago might have looked like. Engineers took advantage of this natural flat valley (the Plain of Ashokan) when they dammed the Esopus Creek to form the reservoir in 1905.

0.00 Jump on your bike, go around the gate, and head west out onto the paved dike.

Immediately, spectacular views open up. Ahead is the Slide Mountain Wilderness Area, and to the right is the Indian Head Wilderness Area.

1.30 At Monument and Reservoir roads, continue heading west on Reservoir Road, passing the aerator on your lower left below the dike (you'll visit it later). There is a wide shoulder and a double line at this point.

1.90 Emerge from the woods onto the main dam. Here you are looking out across the Upper Basin, peering into the high glacial cirque formed by Panther Mountain, Giant Ledge, and the Burroughs Range. Much earlier, the Panther Mountain area was the epicenter of a meteor impact that defined the upper Esopus Valley.

2.60 Cross the main dam.

This is an earthen dam, built at the turn of the century; one of the last ever built by hand (that is, it was constructed using manual labor and steam-powered machines as opposed to being made of formed concrete). This is the point where the Esopus Creek was dammed to form the reservoir. The creek basin can be seen down to the left.

Be careful now as you cross the extremely narrow dam section of the road because of the dam scenery that absorbs drivers (if and when it re-opens to traffic).

2.75 Join NY 28A and turn left. There's a double line with some shoulder. This is a speed zone. Descend.

3.00 Turn left with NY 28A as it passes NY 213 on the right. Be careful at this turn, as road signs are sparse and confusing. This section of NY 28A is not as busy but the shoulder is worse. Coast.

Cyclists relax on the Ashokan's main dike (closed to traffic).

4.30 Cross the Old Esopus Channel in a wild and woodsy setting. This is the buffer zone, so there are no houses.

4.90 Climb through a rich forest of cedar, hemlock, and hardwoods. Only a cinder shoulder exists and sometimes motorists speed through here.

5.10 Cross an old concrete bridge over a spillway channel, and pass the DEP police headquarters on the right at the corner of Beaverkill Road.

5.40 In front of the Ben Nesin Laboratory, bear left onto the aerator circle and pedal around the fountain.

The aerator is no longer used for the oxygen-enrichment of the reservoir water, but it remains as a monument.

5.60 Come out of the circle, and bear left again, and climb to the left up Monument Road, leaving NY 28A.

5.70 Turn right onto the Middle Dike (which you will recognize) and ride east, back to Leonard Hill Circle.

Again, you're treated to fine, extensive views, this time of the Overlook Wild Forest. Overlook Mountain is the farthest to the northeast; it slopes up sharply from the ledge known as Minister's Face and is easily identified by the fire tower (and the ugly cell tower). Beneath Overlook is the town of Woodstock, where Ride 11 begins.

7.00 Pull into Leonard Hill Circle.

If you're returning to the Thruway, by all means take a look at the scenic West Hurley Dike. To do so, bear left out of the circle and set to zero at NY 28A. At 0.6 mile, you'll pass the Spillway. This is a spectacular sight in the early spring when wastewater is channeling its way into the gorge below. At 6.1 miles, leave NY 28A and bear left onto Basin Road (not signed). Within 0.2 miles, you will cross the West Hurley Dike and have another fine view of the Indian Head Wilderness Area, only closer up this time. At 7.3 miles, turn left in front of the Reservoir Inn (great pizza), and at 8.0 miles, turn right onto NY 28. From here you know the way back to the Thruway.

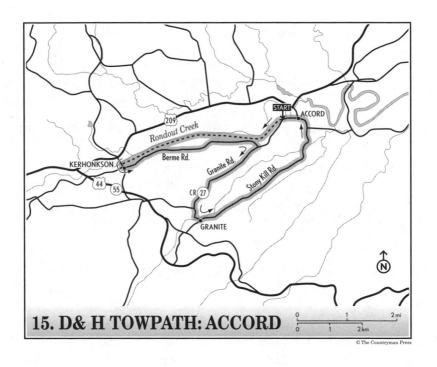

15. D& H TOWPATH: ACCORD

15

The D&H Towpath: Accord

DISTANCE: 12.1 miles

CUMULATIVE ELEVATION GAIN: 550 feet

TERRAIN: Slightly hilly (towpath section is flat)

DIFFICULTY: Easy

RECOMMENDED BICYCLE: Mountain, hybrid

DIRECTIONS

Accord is 16 miles south of New York State Thruway (I-87) Exit 19 (Kingston) on US 209. Turn southeast (left as you're coming south) at the corner of US 209 and CR 27 in Accord. Make the first right on Scenic Road and drive along next to the Rondout Creek for 0.1 mile. Bear right on CR 27, and within 0.1 mile, turn right into the town of Rochester Park and park next to the playground. On the left near the park entrance, you'll see the rail trail.

This short trip along the Rondout Creek and the Delaware and Hudson (D&H) Towpath offers a few options for casual rides. Ride out and back, remaining on the towpath (for a 6.4-mile round trip), or follow a longer route using rural roads to return to your point of origin.

Towpaths were the dirt sidewalks along the edges of canals from which canal barges were pulled, usually by mules or horses, and sometimes by human labor. The canal's existence depended on a large replenishable water source—in this case the Rondout Creek—from which it could be filled to a depth adequate to sustain the heavy coal and freight-laden barges. Water was fed into the canal from the creek by gravity (thus the term *feeder canal*) and had little current. But the terrain was not always level, which necessitated the construction of the elaborate stone locks you can see in the village of High Falls (see Ride 16). Most of the vestigal canal through this area is not obvious. Often, the ditch was a nuisance to farmers, who filled it in, for it was easier than spanning it with bridges. Town roads demolished it. The stones were taken for housing. The ditch filled in naturally with fallen trees and detritus. The later construction of a railbed further obscured any evidence of the towpath or canalway.

The preservation of the towpath and railbed and its development as a recreational route is testimony to the ongoing success of linear park planning in the Hudson Valley. This section was created with Environmental Quality Bond Act project funds in 1986.

0.00 Get on the towpath and head southwest (the only way you can go).

1.50 The Rondout Creek appears on the right. The trail runs through a beautiful hardwood forest and the hard dirt surface improves as you progress.

1.70 The river comes into full view on your right.

2.10 Pass the canoe launch and cross a pair of bridges.

3.20 Pass through a gate. To the left, the canal is full of water, and the hand-laid stone retaining walls are being slowly reclaimed by nature. Now you enter a residential area. (If you want to avoid using roads altogether, return on the towpath.)

3.50 At a point where you reach the Kerhonkson fire station (telephone), go left onto Foordemoore Avenue. On the top of the hill, go left onto Maple Avenue. Turn left onto Berme Road. Pass the town of Rochester rail trail canoe access and picnic area (you can also return this way). Expansive views of the

Catskills develop to the west. Turn right on CR 27 (Granite Road, a.k.a. Upper Granite Road). This is a lined road at this point with a fog line. Traffic is moderate and sometimes fast. Ascend.

8.20 In Granite, at the corner of CR 27 and Lower Granite Road, bear left with CR 27.

8.50 Bear left onto Stony Kill Road. Now you head north to complete the loop. The area is rural. The road surface is loose; mostly dirt.

10.60 Pass Stony Road to your right.

11.10 Cross the Stony Kill.

11.60 Turn left onto Tow Path Road.

11.80 In Accord, note the old Accord station and caboose at the corner of Tobacco Road. Bear left onto CR 27.

12.10 Arrive at the town of Rochester Park.

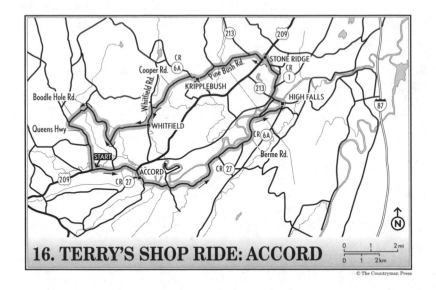

16. TERRY'S SHOP RIDE: ACCORD

Terry's Shop Ride: Accord

DISTANCE: 24.6 miles

CUMULATIVE ELEVATION GAIN: 750 feet

TERRAIN: Hilly

DIFFICULTY: Moderate

RECOMMENDED BICYCLE: Mountain, hybrid, road

DIRECTIONS

Accord is 19 miles south of New York State Thruway (I-87) Exit 19 (Kingston) on US 209. Continue past the tiny hamlet to Terry's Accord Bicycle Service, just before the corner of US 209 and Queens Highway. You can also park in Accord (see Ride 15 for details).

Terry Paddock of the Accord Bicycle Service gave this one to us. This is a variation on one of Terry's shop rides, a route he uses to lead groups in the afternoons during the cycling season. But the old farm roads and byways around the hilly lands of the western Shawangunks and the southern Catskills offer dozens of scenic backroad rides, and Terry will be glad to map out a few for you.

We found this an exhilarating and scenic tour, one that showcases both the rich farm and woodlands of the Rondout Valley and the old berm and restored towpath remnants of the historic Delaware and Hudson Canal (1828) that ran from the Rondout deep into the Pennsylvania coal country. Most of this ride takes place on quiet back roads, but the first section follows US 209, a fairly busy state highway with a good shoulder.

An upscale country store in historic High Falls

0.00 Pull out of the bike shop and turn left (north) on US 209. Get over to the shoulder quickly and stay hard to the right.

0.70 Pass Mettacahonts Road on your left.

1.20 Pass Saunderskill Farm on your left. (Stop in for a visit.)

1.65 Turn right on CR 27 and cross the Rondout Creek. Go straight through Accord village, past the Museum Library and Meeting Room, as well as a municipal parking lot on your left. Continue on CR 27 (a.k.a. Tow Path Road). Following are easy hills and a minimum of traffic. Views of the Catskills develop to the left (west). Passing rows of white pines, through forests of maples, you come to an intersection.

5.45 Bear right on CR 6.

5.55 Bear left.

5.75 Bear left onto Berme Road.

7.80 Pass Stone Dock Road on your left. You're following the old canalway now, and many of the local place-names reflect this.

8.25 Bear right onto Canal Road.

9.15 Bear left on CR 6A (a.k.a. Cedar Hill Road, Mohonk Road) and ride into High Falls.

9.40 At the corner of NY 213 and CR 6A in High Falls, bear left on NY 213. *Take some time to look around this charming little village. Peak into the Depuy Canal House (1876), an intact inn surviving from canal days and functioning as an elegant period restaurant featuring four-star chef John Novi. The Depuy is no longer an inn, but it does house both the Depuy Canal House Restaurant (upstairs, fine dining) and the Chefs On Fire Bistro, serving bistro fare, of course, downstairs. John has always extended his hospitality to those who simply want to take a look at the house, which he purchased in the early '60s.*

When the Delaware and Hudson (D&H) Canal closed in the 1900s, commerce in High Falls also dried up. Today, you can see some of the best-preserved locks of the D&H Canal within a few minutes walk of the Depuy Canal House. (There were five operating locks here.) In fact, one of the best ones is right next to the Depuy. Just across the street on a path accessible to the public, an aqueduct carried barges above the Rondout Creek. What remains of this suspension bridge—designed by John A. Roebling, who later designed the Brooklyn Bridge—can be seen lying in the woods next to the Rondout. The D&H Canal is a national historic landmark, maintained by the D&H Canal Historical Society, which also operates the D&H Canal Museum on CR 6A. The town operates a hydroelectric plant that you'll see on the right as you leave town.

Cross the Rondout Creek now as you travel west on NY 213.

10.00 Turn right at the intersection of CR 1 (Lucas Turnpike) and go uphill. The setting is rural.

10.22 Turn left onto Leggette Road.

10.52 You will pass the Hurley Rail Trail to your right. (For information on the rail trail, see *25 Mountain Bike Tours in the Hudson Valley*.) The area is heavily wooded and gives way to open fields.

11.75 Turn left on US 209. You're in Stone Ridge, now, so there's a bit of local traffic (speed limit 30 mph). Get over to the right and prepare to turn right at the next corner.

11.9 Turn right (west) onto NY 213 (Cooper Street). There's no shoulder but traffic is tame. Pass a cornfield on the right and climb easily.

12.43 Turn left onto Pine Bush Road.
Views to the south open up, including Sky Top tower in the Mohonk Preserve, and eventually you will see the Minnewaska ridge all the way south to the Sam's Point area.

14.72 Go right on Kripplebush Road (CR 2, double lines, no shoulder). Follow it into Kripplebush.

15.00 Turn left onto Cooper Road. The area is quiet, rural, and residential. The road is not lined and there is minimal traffic.

17.00 Turn left onto Whitfield Road.

17.72 Turn right onto Lower Whitfield Road. Traveling west you are again treated to views of the Shawangunks.

19.48 Turn right onto Mettacahonts Road.

21.30 At the end of Mettacahonts Road, turn left onto Boodle Hole Road.

22.30 Turn left on Queens Highway.

24.50 Turn left on US 209.

24.60 Pull into Terry's Accord Bicycle Service.

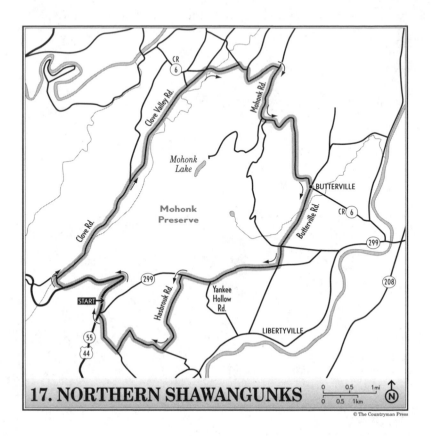

17. NORTHERN SHAWANGUNKS

0   0.5   1mi
0   0.5   1km

N

© The Countryman Press

More Gunk: Around the Northern Shawangunks

DISTANCE: 19.6 miles

CUMULATIVE ELEVATION GAIN: 1950 feet

TERRAIN: Very hilly

DIFFICULTY: Strenuous

RECOMMENDED BICYCLE: Mountain, hybrid, road (no serious dirt unless you shortcut through the Mohonk Preserve)

DIRECTIONS

From Exit 18 of the New York State Thruway (I-87), head west through the village of New Paltz on NY 299 for 7.5 miles. Turn right onto US 44/NY 55 and drive 0.8 mile up the hill to the Mohonk Gateway visitors center. Just beyond the entrance, turn right into the Wawarsing parking area. Arrive early or you won't get a spot. (As a rule, early means before 10 AM on a nice weekend.) If you plan to cut through the Mohonk Preserve (see text), you can purchase a day pass at the visitor center of the Mohonk Mountain House at mile point 9.2.

This ride will introduce you to the scenic northern Shawangunk Ridge and its innumerable delights. You'll encounter the high, white conglomerate cliffs of the Near Trapps, the long and winding forest road of the western clove where the Coxing Kill runs languidly to the Rondout, and cross the hump for the long glide from Mohonk into Butterville.

Have a look at the Mohonk Gateway visitor center at some point, either before or after your tour. It provides a general introduction to the Mohonk Preserve and its ecology, history, and research programs.

There's a gift shop, displays, and a friendly staff who can answer all of your questions about the largest member-supported nature preserve in the state. (If you wish to use the preserve's bike trails, you'll need to purchase a seasonal membership or a day pass, which can be done here or from rangers along the trails.)

0.00 From the Wawarsing parking area, ride up to the main road (US 44/NY 55) and turn right. Stay right, as this road tends to be busy. Traffic seems to be under control but the drivers are sightseeing, so be defensive. There's a large shoulder. Climb through the hairpin turn and ascend beneath the Trapps.

Views of the valley are outstanding from the 20-minute parking area on the left. Pass the rock climber's camping area on the left before the bridge.

0.75 Pass under Trapps Bridge and Trapps Carriageway, part of the vast carriageway and hiking/biking system of the Gunks (see Ride 18). Descend, passing the West Trapps parking area (fee, but free for members or with purchase of day pass).

1.30 Turn right onto Clove Road (no shoulders, no lines). This woodsy back road follows along the edge of the Coxing Kill.

1.60 Bear right at the fork.

2.30 Pass the Coxing entry parking area on the left.

This is an access point to the Mohonk Preserve and hotel grounds via the Old Minnewaska Road. It is also the site of an early farmstead. A day pass will allow you to swim at Split Rock, a large crevice located on the kill, just a few minute's walk along the trail. If you're so inclined, farther down the Coxing Kill, there's a nude sunbathing area. Signs will alert you to NUDISM AHEAD. There's normally a staff member at the parking area that can fill you in.

You draw away from the Coxing Kill now and into its scenic valley, riding up and down with views of the Outback Slabs area of the western Shawangunk Ridge on your right. The shoulder is gravelly, and there's little traffic. The ridge begins to taper down and there are a few long downhills.

5.85 Go straight at an intersection with Clove Valley Extension, remaining on Clove Road.

6.35 Bear right onto CR 6 (a.k.a. Clove Valley Road) in front of a beautiful, Dutch-style stone house. This is a lined county road with no shoulders, but it's a short section.

A pair of cycle tourists relax along a road in the Gunks.

6.50 Cross the Coxing Kill for the last time. The shoulder improves. There's a gravel-covered fog line. The setting is still rural.

6.60 Now you begin to earn some elevation as the road rises to pass the very tempting Old Clove Road on your left.

7.10 At a stop sign and intersection with CR 6A (Mohonk Road), bear right on CR 6 (also Mohonk Road) and granny down for a cruel and belittling ascent. Climb up a long switchback into the northeast, featuring unbelievable views to the northwest that improve with elevation (as they all seem to do).

Those are the Catskills in the distance. Spring Farm—one of the Gunks most coveted sylvan dales, lies below. Between it and the far hills are the fecund emerald valleys of the Rondout and Esopus. Many carriageway systems appear in the vicinity through here, all of them penetrating the heart of the preserve. Some are open to bikes (entry fee applies).

The road makes a long straightaway and the traffic sometimes moves fast, so pay attention to that, too.

8.20 Pass Upper 27 Knolls Road on your left. There's a trailhead parking area a short way in, with carriageway and foot trail access. Keep going on Mohonk Road. The climb intensifies now.

You're climbing the western shoulder of Guyot Hill (named for Princeton geologist and founder of the United States Weather Service, Arnold Guyot, who measured all the Catskill peaks).

9.20 Gasping, you top out at the gatehouse of the Mohonk Mountain House. The golf course is on your left.

The gatehouse staff is a friendly bunch. You can use the rest room here, buy a coke or a day pass, or get a drink at the water fountain. You can purchase a day pass and shortcut this tour if you wish, by using the bike-legal (dirt) carriageway that heads west back to the Trapps. (You really have to try this sometime. Should you like to try it now, we highly recommend that you take Lenape Lane to Oakwood Drive to Undercliff Road to Trapps Bridge. The gatehouse can provide bike maps and assistance.)

Adjust your gear and secure everything, you've got a long fast downhill ahead on Mountain Rest Road (the continuation of Mohonk Road).

10.8 Cross the Catskill Aqueduct, which carries water from the Catskills to New York City.

11.40 Arrive at Butterville Corners, a four-way intersection. Go right onto Butterville Road. You'll pass several open landscapes with a viewshed of Sky Top and the upper realms of the Mohonk Preserve for the next 1.5 miles.

12.50 Go under the Mohonk Gatehouse Road. (This was the original approach to the Mohonk Mountain House.)

12.80 At this intersection of Butterville Road and NY 299, bear right and follow NY 299 west. Pass the Leuken Orchards (excellent apple cider and snacks) at the corner of Yankee Folly Road. Stay hard right on NY 299, the shoulders are poor and traffic can be fast—but many cyclists use this road.

15.25 Turn left on Hasbrouk Road (to cut out the worst section of NY 299).

16.80 Turn right on Guilford Schoolhouse Road (a.k.a. Schoolhouse Road,

Guilford Mountain Road).

17.60 Bear left at Marakill Road (named for the Mara Kill Creek), remaining on Guilford Schoolhouse Road.

18.00 Bear right on Guilford Mountain Road and ascend steeply.

18.70 Turn right onto US 44/NY 55, leave NY 299 to your right, and ascend.

19.60 Arrive at the Mohonk Gateway visitor center and Wawarsing parking area.

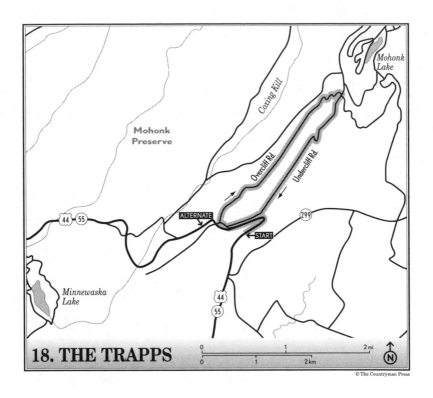

18. THE TRAPPS

© The Countryman Press

Hard Rock: The Trapps

DISTANCE: 4.8 miles

CUMULATIVE ELEVATION GAIN: 300 feet

TERRAIN: Mostly flat, one small hill

DIFFICULTY: Easy

RECOMMENDED BICYCLE: Mountain, hybrid

DIRECTIONS

From Exit 18 of the New York State Thruway (I-87), head west through the village of New Paltz on NY 299 for 7.5 miles. Turn right onto US 44/NY 55 and drive 0.8 mile up the hill to the Mohonk Gateway visitor center. Just beyond the entrance, turn right into the Wawarsing parking area. Arrive early or you won't get a spot (as a rule of thumb, early means before 10 AM on a nice weekend). If you can't get a spot here, continue on US 44/NY55 to the West Trapps parking area (fee) just beyond Trapps Bridge on the right. From either the West Trapps or Wawarsing parking areas, ride up to Trapps Bridge. (This will mean coming up US 44/NY 55 from the Wawarsing lot. See Ride 17 for additional details.) The West Trapps lot is preferable because you can reach Trapps Bridge without riding in the road.

Here's an introduction to the carriage road system of the Shawangunks, which connects the Mohonk Preserve to Minnewaska State Park. Most of these stone carriage roads were laid down up to two hundred years ago by the Smiley brothers, the Quaker farmers who got into the hotel business to pay the taxes on their vast holdings on the Shawangunk Ridge. They realized that they owned a special piece of creation, and rather than sell it off to conserve a smaller nucleus, they went commercial to preserve the entire piece. And they did so with elegance and refinement, as anyone who visits the Mohonk Mountain House will attest.

The carriage roads are in fact similar in width and construction to back roads—these were the forest routes used by the Smileys to delight their guests by horse-drawn carriage. They have stood up so well over time because they are covered with the durable shale that overlays the white quartz conglomerate bedrock of the ridge. Carriage roads are so roadlike in construction and gradient that they can be ridden by hybrids with no problem whatsoever. But the loose Martinsburg shale will quickly frustrate skinny-tired touring cyclists.

This tour will take you around 5 miles of what is probably the most popular multi-use carriage route in the Shawangunks. (There are 29 miles of carriage roads in the Mohonk Preserve, and a total of about 100 miles including Minnewaska State Park.) It can be argued that the hiking and biking routes to Castle Point in Minnewaska are busier on any given weekend. They offer both stunning viewsheds from Castle and Hamilton points and the sky lakes swimming beaches at Lake Awosting and Minnewaska (see *25 Mountain Bike Tours in the Hudson Valley* for details). In contrast, the Trapps carriage roads hold the pedigree on Gunks' grandeur and mystique, not only for the considerable natural beauty of the Trapps' fascinating talus and cliff environment, but because this is the nerve center of North American rock climbing. Thus, people from all walks of life and every corner of the globe converge on the Uberfall to try a few of the Gunks' one thousand climbing routes. This atmosphere draws its onlookers, well-wishers, and amazed wanna-bees, of course. The sport of technical rock climbing is no less colorful than any other, with its sparkling hardware, multicolored ropes, and dedicated apparel; a fully outfitted climber may be carrying gear that's worth as much as your BMW. But you'll find that it doesn't require a great deal to get involved in this thrilling sport, and local guides will show you how, starting with some of the basic climbs that you will be able to see as you cycle along. (Ask any ranger for information.)

0.00 From Trapps Bridge, head north, bearing left at the fork onto Overcliff Road (a.k.a. Carriage Road).

The road winds in and out of the woods, offering westerly views, first of the immediate hills and ledges above the Coxing Kill Valley, among them Rock Hill, Dickie Barre, and Ronde Barre. This is the ridge that separates the Coxing Kill from the Rondout Valley.

Undercliff Road is among the Gunks' most popular cycling paths.

The road is level as you come out onto the west-facing slope of the Trapps. Low angled slabs retreat downhill to the west and climb on your right. Far-reaching views of the Catskills begin with Ashokan High Point in the southwest and reach through the High Peaks area and north. Pitch pines and blueberry heaths dot the landscape. You'll encounter many hikers, so yield the right-of-way.

1.90 Toward the north end, Overcliff Road takes a turn to the northeast and begins a slight descent, dropping down through the north end of the tapering Trapps scarp and arriving among the laurel slicks of Rhododendron Bridge. Here, Oakwood Drive, Old Minnewaska Road, and Laurel Ledge Road come together. What a pretty spot this is!

2.4 From Rhododendron Bridge, bear right onto Undercliff Road and wind your way through the dense oak forests toward the cliffs.

3.10 Now you draw close beneath the high vertical face of the Trapps, with 250 feet of vertical rise, but the Carriage Road is flat. From this point forward you will encounter climbers, their numbers increasing as you draw nearer to the Uberfall.

4.40 Arrive at the Uberfall, the general meeting place in the Trapps, where there's a map and information kiosk and rest rooms.

Normally, a ranger is posted here. Rangers are well versed in the art of climbing, and they operate a first aid station and conduct search and rescue. Now you will probably want to walk your bike, because the carriage road is so busy or because you'll want to pause and watch climbers. Don't distract the belaying partners, however, who are standing below the cliffs and working with a partner on the rock. They keep in constant contact verbally and are often joined together by a top rope. Clear communication is critical, and instruction and advice is being shared often. The atmosphere is solemn.

4.80 Continue around the southeast end of the cliffs and climb a bit to Trapps Bridge.

For more information about the Mohonk Preserve and its programs, policies, and membership plans, and to learn more about the resource, by all means visit the Gateway visitor center. To learn more about climbing, visit the infamous Rock and Snow on Main Street in New Paltz, and pick up a copy of Dick Williams' The Gunks Select—The Definitive Guide to the Best Rock Climbing Routes in the Shawangunks.

19

Might As Well Jump: New Paltz

DISTANCE: 17 miles

CUMULATIVE ELEVATION GAIN: 533 feet

TERRAIN: Slightly hilly

DIFFICULTY: Moderate

RECOMMENDED BICYCLE: Mountain, hybrid, road

DIRECTIONS

From Exit 18 of the New York State Thruway (I-87), head west into the village of New Paltz on NY 299. Cross Chestnut Street (NY 32). Just before the Wallkill River Bridge, at the bottom (west end) of the village, you'll cross the Wallkill Valley Rail Trail. You'll notice several parking spots nearby (try to use the one immediately to the left) that may be full on weekends. If that's the case, turn right on Huguenot Street where there's a public park ahead (take the first left). Ride back to the NY 299 rail trail crosswalk to begin.

There is an oft-quoted fairy tale that the city of Oxford, England once had so many bicycles that the good citizenry lost track of their own respective bikes, so simply shared them all. If you needed a bike, you just grabbed one and rode it to your destination. The other bloke would take yours—if he could find it. And if you go to Oxford, which aside from Montreal may seem like the bike-friendliest city on earth, you might even believe it. The City of Spires paints a romanticized picture of bespectacled, baguette-toting business folk riding bicycles by the thousands, commingling with sympathetic automobile traffic in one big, happy parade. So what if you can't treat the bikes in New Paltz as

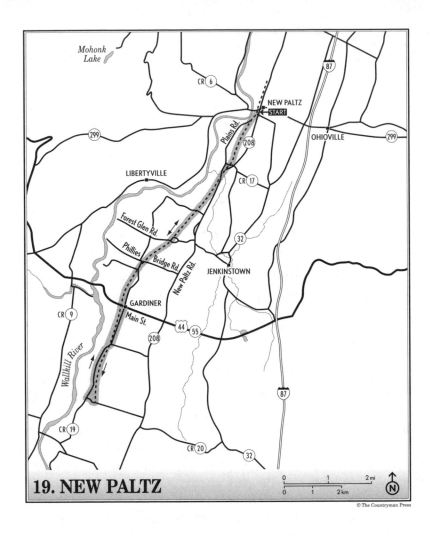

19. NEW PALTZ

© The Countryman Press

communal property without making the acquaintance of the notorious local constabulary? You can still join in the ride here in the Hudson Valley's bike-friendliest town (feel free to quote us on that), taking time to visit the area's 100 miles of carriage roads, 12 miles of rail trail, and no less than three local bike shops. The aorta of the New Paltz bike world is the Wallkill Valley Rail Trail that runs through the middle of town. This is where the ride begins.

0.00 At the pedestrian crosswalk provided for rail trail users, you'll see a sign identifying the Wallkill Valley Rail Trail.

On the southeast side of this corner is the Water Street Antique and Art Village, where you can also get tourist information. A train station sits to the north on the rail trail, at this time housing an Italian restaurant. There are views to the west of the Shawangunk Ridge, including Sky Top, Millbrook Mountain, and the Trapps.

Pedal south, with the antique village on the left, and follow the gravel rail trail, immediately crossing Plains Road into the woods. The Wallkill River is visible on your right.

0.25 A nameless backwater creek comes into the river at a point where a set of stairs leads down to its edge.

You can follow it if you like; it returns to the rail trail again just ahead. The trail is a very wide double track cinder surface. Cross Plains Road again, which is sometimes nearly tunneled in by vegetation (depending on trail maintenance).

1.60 Cross Cedar Lane. The path is lined with little locust trees and trout lilies.

1.80 At the end of Plains Road, continue on the rail trail.

1.90 Cross a pretty creek on a high bridge enclosed by a chain-link fence.

There is a farm below, with a stream, cows, sycamore trees, and a broad viewshed. The Trapps loom, shining in white above Undercliff Carriageway. The trail becomes wilder and narrower after this and views to the west continue.

2.40 Cross a private farm road with a substantial orchard, both left and right, and more great views.

3.00 Cross Old Ford Road.

3.90 Cross Bridge Creek Road; you're still in farm country.

4.00 Cross a bridge over Forest Glen Road. The surface is still good, but in some sections gravel yields to dirt and the width reduces to a single track with some ballast chunks that *twang* under your tires.

4.90 Cross Phillies Bridge Road at the corner of Old Ford Road. You can see where the rails go under the road. Keep your eyes open for skydivers in the southeast.

5.10 Cross Steve's Lane.

6.10 Cross Main Street (US 44/NY 55) in the town of Gardiner.
This is an interesting place to look around. There are a couple of antiques stores, a deli, and a pizzeria.

Follow the rail trail south and cross Farmer's Turnpike. Now the trail widens.
You may see up to a dozen sport jumpers at a time from here, but you will pass right by the airstrip on the way back north where you can take a closer look.

7.30 Cross Sand Hill Road.

7.80 Cross an unidentified gravel road.

8.70 Denniston Road. This is the end of the trail. Turn right.

9.00 At Sand Hill Road (CR 19), turn right (no shoulder, centerline, or fog line). There are views of the Shawangunks to left, west and north. Millbrook is the large face diagonally to the north (left). Pass a tree farm on the left.

10.30 Cross the rail trail again.

11.10 The Ranch parachute club appears on the right. Continue north on Sand Hill Road.
The parachute club invites the curious to inquire. If you're interested and arrive early, you can jump the same day, but reservations are suggested. You must be under 225 pounds (generally) and at least 18 years of age. Preparations for your first jump involve watching a video and filling out papers. You don't need insurance—you are jumping at your own risk. You can be in the air within an hour of your arrival. After five jumps you can do a solo sky dive. The standard jump height is 13,500 feet. After that jumps are cheaper. Many of the jumpers you will meet at the club have logged several hundred jumps.

11.30 Turn left on US 44/NY 55 in Gardiner.

11.40 Turn right on the Wallkill Valley Rail Trail and return to New Paltz.
We didn't jump. Did you? If you didn't either, you may still have time to ride along Huguenot Street in the historic district of New Paltz. Huguenot Street is the western-most street before the Wallkill River on the north side of Main Street (NY 299). On lands purchased from the Esopus Indians (Gee, where have we heard this before?), the Duzine, a group of religious refugees (Palatines), built die Pfaltz, a small community of

farms that is said to be on the oldest street in the United States that still has its original houses. These beautiful homes, maintained by the venerable Huguenot Historical Society, date—unbelievably enough—from 1692. And these were the renovations that re-placed even earlier huts and log houses. The homes are open for tours after Memorial Day through Labor Day. For information call 845-255-1889.

The Wallkill Valley Rail Trail was created through a huge volunteer effort coordinated by the Wallkill Valley Rail Trail Association (WVRTA). Become a member and join the fun! For information about this unique linear greenway, write WVRTA, PO Box 1048, New Paltz, NY, 12561.

II. EAST OF THE HUDSON

Relaxing at Poet's Walk romantic landscape park

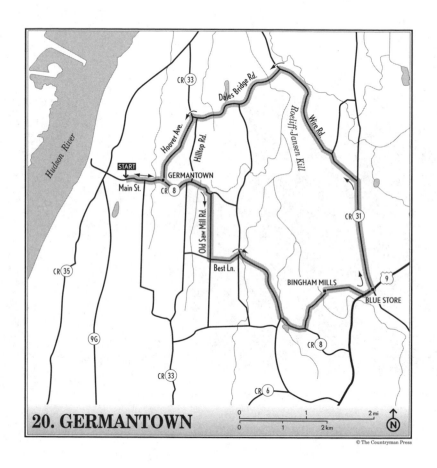

20. GERMANTOWN

20

Auf Wiedersehen: Germantown

DISTANCE: 13 miles

CUMULATIVE ELEVATION GAIN: 411 feet

TERRAIN: Rolling

DIFFICULTY: Moderate

RECOMMENDED BICYCLE: Mountain, hybrid, road

DIRECTIONS

From the corner of NY 9G and NY 199, 3 miles east of the Kingston-Rhinecliff Bridge toll plaza, on the border of the Rhinebeck and Red Hook village limits, set to zero and go north on NY 9G. In 3.5 miles, pass the entrance to Bard College on the left. At 6 miles pass CR 78 (you would take this left for Ride 28) and continue north on NY 9G, passing the sign for the Clermont State Historic Site at 7.8 miles. At 11.5 miles turn right onto CR 8. This will bring you to Palatine Park within 0.3 mile. Turn left onto the park road and continue to the picnic area, where you can find a good parking spot.

Germantown is named for the Palatines who settled here in great numbers as early as 1710. They came against their will as subjects and servants of England, whose Queen Anne promised them lands in exchange for labor. They were charged with producing tar from pine trees to support Britain's production of naval stores (those ships leaked a lot), over which Sweden held a monopoly. Not wishing to rely on a single source for the needs of their growing navy, the English hatched a plan to turn these religious refugees into a tar-production workforce. The plan ultimately failed, and the Palatines were released of their obligations but given none of the lands they were promised.

They became farmers, primarily, settling in the Hudson River counties of Columbia, Dutchess, and Ulster. There was a large encampment of Palatines on both sides of the river here, thus the place-names East Camp (in Columbia) and West Camp (in Ulster). The farms and kills of this easy backroad tour remain as part of many early Palatine settlements and pre-Revolutionary homesteads, mostly on the extensive real estate holdings of the Livingston family. At one time the Livingstons held more than a million acres in the Hudson Valley, including huge blocks in the Catskills' Hardenburgh Patent and what amounted to nearly a third of Dutchess County. As you ride the easy hills and flats that came at such a price to those who cleared it long ago, you will marvel and rejoice in the bounty of this rich agricultural land.

0.00 From Palatine Park, head back out to CR 8. This is the location of an austere-looking, yellowish town hall, solid waste station, and community and youth activity building. (Who on earth picked the color?) Turn left onto Main Street (CR 8).

0.60 Come into the tiny village of Germantown. There is a small store here. Proceed through town. CR 8 is lined and not heavily trafficked.

1.20 Crest a hill and begin downhill, as the scenery becomes rural.

1.40 Pass Hilltop Road on the left.
This is a pretty farm area of open fields and old homes. You will pass the home of Diell Rockefeller, one of the original Palatine settlers who landed at East Camp in 1733. Juniper thickets and hardwood hillocks characterize the land.

1.40 Turn right on Old Saw Mill Road.

2.40 Turn left on Best Lane.

2.80 Join CR 8 at the intersection of South Road. Continue on CR 8.

4.50 At a T, turn left on Mill Road, going northeast. There are no lines on this road.

5.10 Bingham Mills. Cross the Roeliff-Jansen Kill at the site of an old, washed-out dam. This river is a very popular white-water run. Bear right, remaining on Mill Road. Go through big orchards and open fields where the road is lined with sugar maples. This end of the road is Bingham Mills Road. Turn left onto US 9 and go a short distance north. Turn left onto CR 31 (Highland Turnpike) in Blue Stores.

This is the site of an early store owned by Walter Livingston, which included a blue store and tavern. Some say the place was named after the store's color (blue, of course), others say it was for nearby Blue Hill, and still others say both reasons are true. Go uphill. The road levels out in expansive, open fields with far-reaching views. The conspicuous knob to the north is Blue Hill.

7.50 Turn left onto Wire Road.

This is the location of a high plateau, where all you can see is a few farms among the fields. There are views of the Catskills from here at what is perhaps the highlight viewshed area of the tour.

9.50 Pass Teviotdale (built in 1774).

Teviotdale was once the estate of Walter Livingston, and one of whose daughters married steamboat inventor Robert Fulton (1765–1815). The Fultons lived here from 1808 until shortly after Robert Fulton's death. This imposing, pre-Revolutionary, block-style mansion in the Georgian Federal style is set in fields off the road in full view of passers-by, and it is privately owned today. Teviotdale is the former name for an area of Great Britain and the southern uplands of Scotland (the first Livingstons came from Scotland) where the rivers Teviot and Tweed flow to the North Sea. That area (now known as the Borders because it lies between England and Scotland) is characterized by rolling hills and rushing rivers, hemmed by hardwood-covered flatlands and pastures. Like the Teviotdale of old, this Teviotdale was also populated with sheep. You will know why Livingston named the area for his hilly ancestral homeland as soon as you make the sharp descent ahead to cross the Roeliff-Jansen Kill. This is perhaps the hilliest part of the county (but they're small hills).

9.60 Turn left onto Dales Bridge Road. Descend steeply now, crossing the Roeliff-Jansen Kill. This is the Livingston-Germantown line (established in 1788). Now you're in North Germantown, climbing hard.

10.70 Eastern Parkway (a misnomer) comes in from the left at the site of Mountain Range Farm.

11.00 Pass Hilltop Road on the left.

11.30 Turn left onto Hoover Avenue (CR 33, speed limit 45 mph). Go downhill to CR 8.

12.40 Turn right (west) onto CR 8 and go through Germantown.

13.00 Arrive back at the entrance to Palatine Park.

21

You Name It: Philmont

DISTANCE: 15.6 miles

CUMULATIVE ELEVATION GAIN: 1230 feet

TERRAIN: Rolling

DIFFICULTY: Moderate

RECOMMENDED BICYCLE: Mountain, hybrid

DIRECTIONS

Philmont is 8 miles east of Hudson on NY 217 and 2 miles west of the Taconic State Parkway's Philmont exit. Park in Claverack Town Park, just off Church Street in the village of Philmont. Other than providing a place to leave your car for the day, the park has few amenities for cyclists, no shade (except for a picnic area in the pavilion), and no scenery. It is also possible to park almost anywhere in the village on NY 217. Provisions are available in several markets and convenience stores.

Philmont lies in the gently rolling farm country of central Columbia County, equidistant between the Hudson River and the southern Taconic range of mountains. Because of its extensive farms, a good deal of the land is uninhabited and wild, and most of the back roads are dirt.

0.00 Leave the town park and turn left onto Church Street.

0.50 Turn left on NY 217 and go to the next intersection.

0.60 Turn left on Maple Street. This is a pleasant residential street with no lines and little traffic. Eventually the setting becomes rural; the road descends into

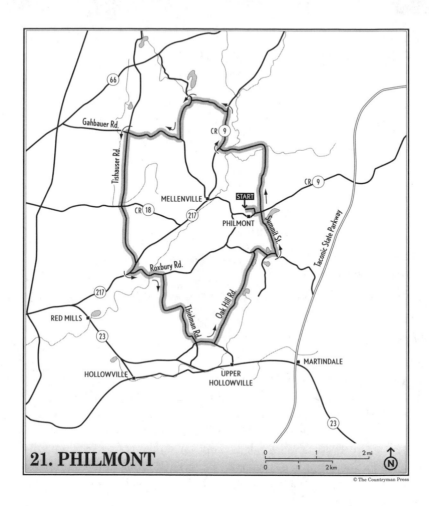

21. PHILMONT

0   1   2 mi
0   1   2 km

© The Countryman Press

the township of Ghent and breaks out into open fields and pasturelands. Cross North Creek.

2.70 Turn right onto the Ghent-Mellenville Road (CR 9), taking care to keep far right. Traffic is for some reason unforgiving, but sight distance is good and there is a soft bailout shoulder. This is the only difficult road on the tour.

3.50 Turn left on Winters Hill Road and ascend. This scenic road levels out at mile 3.8.

4.30 Turn left on Ostrander Road (dirt).

5.10 Go right on Gahbauer Road. This is a lined road with a minimal but useful shoulder that gradually improves.

6.20 At Tishauser Road, turn left. The road is paved but unlined. Big fields, rolling hills, farms, and distant stands of spruce and hardwood make this a very attractive setting.

7.60 Cross CR 18 (Fish and Game Road), continuing on Tishauser Road. The road runs along the west slope of a low ridge, offering startling views of the Catskill Mountains around mile 8.

8.80 Turn right onto NY 217 for a short distance.

9.00 Turn left onto Roxbury Road (paved and unlined).

9.40 Cross Hollowville (Claverack) Creek.

9.60 Turn right onto Thielman Road (dirt). The area is heavily wooded. Soon the road turns to pavement.

11.50 At a point where the road crests a small rise, views to the south appear and you arrive at an intersection.

11.60 Bear left onto (gravel, dirt) Old Barrington Road.

11.80 At an intersection in dense woods, go left onto Oak Hill Road and climb. At some points, this road is almost tunneled over in oak. A long descent follows. Pass Moore Pond, which is barely visible through the woods to the right (east).

13.70 At Steevers Crossing Road, turn right. There's a pretty farm pond on the right before the intersection. Climb a bit.

14.20 Turn left on Summit Street and work your way into the village. Come downhill, past the falls and millpond. The mill is on your left.

15.00 Bear right, remaining on Summit Street.

15.10 Turn left on NY 217, in front of St. Mary's Episcopal Church.

15.20 Turn right on Church Street.

15.70 Arrive at Claverack Town Park.

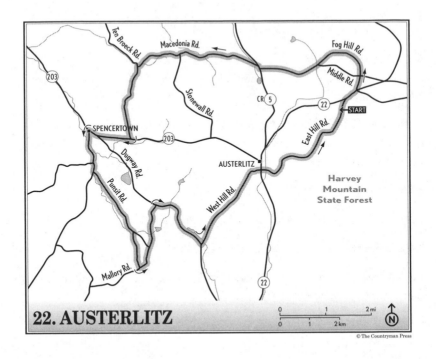

22. AUSTERLITZ

Ten Broeck Rd.

Macedonia Rd.

Fog Hill Rd.

Middle Rd

203

Stonewall Rd.

CR 5

22

START

SPENCERTOWN

203

Dugway Rd.

AUSTERLITZ

East Hill Rd.

Punsit Rd.

West Hill Rd.

Harvey
Mountain
State Forest

Mallory Rd.

22

0   1   2 mi
0   1   2 km

N

The Poetry Trail: Austerlitz

DISTANCE: 19.7 miles

CUMULATIVE ELEVATION GAIN: 2600 feet

TERRAIN: Hilly

DIFFICULTY: Strenuous

RECOMMENDED BICYCLE: Mountain, hybrid

DIRECTIONS

At the corner of NY 22 and East Hill Road in the town of Austerlitz, you'll find the Austerlitz post office and a historical signpost commemorating Steepletop, the home and working place of Edna St. Vincent Millay. Turn east on East Hill Road, passing Steepletop at 2 miles. At 2.3 miles, pass the Millay Poetry Trail. At 2.5 miles, park on the left in the Harvey Mountain State Forest parking area. There's free camping along Bald Mountain Road opposite the parking area.

Tucked into the corner of the county's western woodlands—at the seeming edge of the world—is Austerlitz (1750), a fascinating hinterland of rambling farms, little-used state forests, and bucolic back roads. The thing we like about this area is that you can still find free camping in either of two state forests at a time when the nearest state campground (Taconic State Park at Bash Bish Falls) is charging $18 a night for a place to pitch a tent (of course, they have showers). If you were cycling cross-country, these little state forests are where you could camp each night, at the edge of ponds, in the deepest woods, unseen and undetected. As it is, you can drive right to the legal, designated campsites in Harvey Mountain State Forest and even the ones at Beebe Hill (perhaps with a little more difficulty and ideally a four-wheel-drive vehicle). The opportunity to camp makes it a little more practical to ride Steepletop and Canaan, two relatively remote destinations in northern Columbia County. It's a long way for most people to come just for a day—and it's a place that merits more than a day's stay.

0.00 Head out of the parking lot and turn left (north) onto East Hill Road.

0.40 Turn right onto NY 22.

0.70 Turn left onto Fog Hill Road (dirt).

1.00 Go through the intersection of Fog Hill and Middle Road. Continue straight.

You're traveling under the southern slopes of Fog Hill, into the lands of Beebe Hill State Forest. The bulk of the state forest is on the west side of CR 5. To the left and across CR 5 at this point is Barrett Pond, a quiet and pleasant place to visit. Trails in this section of the forest lead to Beebe Hill and the fire tower. There's free camping in the area (look for designated yellow CAMPING ALLOWED discs).

2.44 Leave Middle Road to your left.

3.70 At the intersection of Fog Hill Road and CR 5, bear right.

3.80 Turn left onto Macedonia Road, a beautiful but fairly rough dirt road.

5.50 Pass Stonewall Road on your right. Continue straight ahead, leaving Stonewall Road to your left at 5.6 miles.

6.00 At the corner of Reed and Ten Broeck Roads, turn left.

7.30 The road turns to pavement.

8.60 Arrive at NY 203. Turn right (west). Go downhill, keeping hard to the right on a marginal shoulder (speed limit 40 mph).

9.50 Enter the quaint colonial crossroads of Spencertown. There's a small country store here. Get on CR 7 now, heading south.

10.30 Turn left on Punsit Road, an unlined, paved road over rolling hills, and pass open fields (road turns to dirt).

12.40 Turn left onto Mallory Road at the site of an elegant old farm.

13.40 Turn right on Dugway Road. Cultivated fields and views to the east follow.

14.90 Turn left on West Hill Road. Climb and then enjoy a long, beautifully wooded descent.

17.10 Arrive at NY 22 and the intersection with East Hill Road.

Just outside Harvey Mountain State Forest, on East Hill Road (walk a few hundred yards west of the trailhead parking area) and along the upper fringes of Steepletop, is the Millay Poetry Trail, a short walk posted with selections of Edna St. Vincent Millay's nature poetry from 1917–1935. (Millay won a Pulitzer for her collection The Harp Weaver and Other Poems *and was noted for her sonnets.) This short trail (about 0.4 mile) leads through quiet woods to her grave and the graves of her mother, Cora Millay, and her husband, Eugen Jan Boissevain. There's a sign and parking area. The Millay Colony for the Arts, established by the poet's sister Norma, is an active artist-in-residence colony. The poet lived here between 1920 and 1950. Apparently, she liked to ride a bicycle through these remote mountain roads.*

Each summer, Austerlitz holds its Blueberry Festival. In autumn, it conducts a community living history festival called Autumn in Austerlitz, when citizens dress up in 1830s period dress at old Austerlitz Village. For information, go to www.oldausterlitz.org.

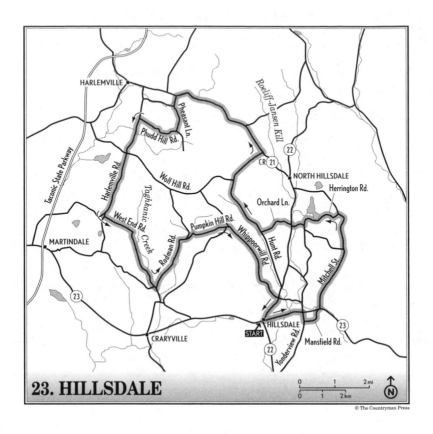

HARLEMVILLE

Pheasant Ln.

Phudd Hill Rd.

Roeliff-Jansen Kill

CR 21

22

Taconic State Parkway

Wolf Hill Rd.

NORTH HILLSDALE

Herrington Rd.

Harlemville Rd.

Taghkanic Creek

West End Rd.

Orchard Ln.

Rodman Rd.

Pumpkin Hill Rd.

Whippoorwill Rd.

Hunt Rd.

Mitchell St.

MARTINDALE

23

START HILLSDALE

23

CRARYVILLE

Yonderview Rd.

Mansfield Rd.

22

23. HILLSDALE

0   1   2 mi
0   1   2 km

N

© The Countryman Press

All This Useless Beauty: Hillsdale

DISTANCE: Loop A, 27.4 miles; Loop B, 25.2 miles

CUMULATIVE ELEVATION GAIN: Loop A, 2300 feet; Loop B, 1900 feet

TERRAIN: Hilly

DIFFICULTY: Strenuous

RECOMMENDED BICYCLE: Mountain, hybrid

DIRECTIONS

Hillsdale lies at the corners of NY 23 and NY 22 in Columbia County, 17 miles north of Millerton (NY 22) and 7 miles east of the Taconic State Parkway at Martindale (NY 23). You can look out across the sweeping amber fields and seasoned farms of Hillsdale and find yourself bewitched into lofty considerations of the endlessness of open space, of the nature and origins of picturesque landscapes, and of the impossible detail in tended heirloom fields with precisely spaced furrows. Everything (from a distance) appears so orderly and manicured. Here is a Hobbitian world of old stone homes tucked into dark woods. A culture of blood-red barns, milky white farmsteads, fowl-muddied ponds, tomato-speckled kitchen gardens, and cordially waving clotheslines that only the silent cyclist seems privy to. Quietly gliding on rubber tires amid the alfalfa fields, you are a spy upon nature and the goings on of agrarians, a cataloger of woodland wealth, and an anonymous witness to the inner workings of the sylvan world.

Many visitors to Hillsdale come for the well-known Falcon Ridge Folk Festival that takes place each July (for the last 18 years). The festival is touted as "a four-day community of folk music and dance at the foot of the Berkshires." In the past this event has featured stage concerts, camping, crafts, workshops, song swaps, activities for kids, an emerging artist showcase, and over 50 acts on four stages. In the wood-floored dance tent, there are contra and square, swing and lindy hop, zydeco, polka, family, and gender-free dances. On-site camping is available. Volunteers get free admission and meals. Locations vary. For information go to www.FalconRidgeFolk.com.

0.00 Begin at the Hillsdale Community Park, hidden in the southwest corner of the intersection of NY 23/22 on Maple Street. Head east on NY 23. This is a busy intersection so be careful. There's a paved shoulder.

1.10 Turn right on Yonderview Road.

1.35 Go left on Mansfield Road. Come downhill to NY 23. Be careful, the road is blind to the left.

2.00 Cross NY 23 onto unlined Mitchell Street. This is a very wooded area. The road surface is patched tar.

4.90 Turn left on Herrington Road. The surface is dirt. Descend.

5.50 Pass Herrington Pond on the right and an emerging marsh on the left.

6.10 Turn right onto Collins Street and cross the Roeliff-Jansen Kill.

6.40 At NY 22, bear right.

6.45 Turn left on Orchard Lane (paved, no lines).

6.90 The road turns to dirt.

7.40 Turn right on Hunt Road (no lines or shoulder). You'll see red-winged blackbirds and a Holstein farm.

9.10 Pass Wolf Hill Road on your left.

10.20 At CR 21, turn left. This is a relatively dull stretch of road, but you can go fast. It's not too busy. There's a small, loose shoulder. You've been climbing steadily between Lyon Mountain and Pumpkin Hill, but not steeply. Following a descent, the shoulder improves.

13.40 Turn left on Pheasant Lane and climb. This is the backcountry.

14.40 At Phudd Hill Road, turn right. This is a very rural area with few houses.

15.70 Turn left onto Harlemville Road.

16.60 Continue straight through a four corners (the corner of Wolf Hill Road and Harlemville Road), at the site of a graveyard (Crum Church cemetery).

17.15 Philmont Reservoir appears to the right.

18.50 Turn left onto West End Road (paved).

19.40 Cross the Taghkanic Creek.

21.20 Turn left on Rodman Road and climb, leveling through Knapp Hollow. The road is mainly dirt but turns to pavement here and there.

22.90 Turn right on Pumpkin Hill Road (dirt) and climb. The dirt surface degenerates.

24.20 Turn right onto Whippoorwill Road (a.k.a. Sharts Street) and head downhill. There are sustained, beautiful views of the Taconic plateau ahead.

26.80 Turn right on NY 22. Stay to the right—the shoulder is wide.

27.40 Arrive back at the intersection of NY 23 and NY 22. What there is of the village of Hillsdale is located to the west on NY 23.

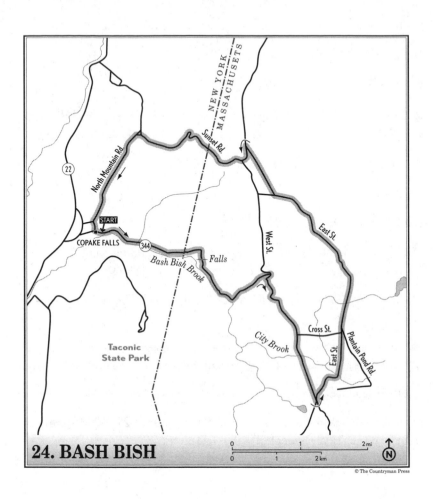

NEW YORK
MASSACHUSETTS

22

North Mountain Rd.

Sunset Rd.

START
COPAKE FALLS

344

Bash Bish Brook

Falls

West St.

East St.

Cross St.

City Brook

East St.

Plantain Pond Rd.

Taconic
State Park

24. BASH BISH

0   1   2 mi
0   1   2 km

N

© The Countryman Press

After the Fall: Bash Bish

DISTANCE: 12.5 miles

CUMULATIVE ELEVATION GAIN: 1800 feet

TERRAIN: Hilly

DIFFICULTY: Strenuous

RECOMMENDED BICYCLE: Mountain, hybrid (some dirt)

DIRECTIONS

From the intersection of NY 22 and NY 344 in Copake Falls, New York, turn east (right, if you're coming north) onto NY 344 and go 0.5 mile to the Harlem Valley Rail Trail (HVRT) parking area. Park on the left in the designated HVRT parking lot. From the Taconic State Parkway, exit onto NY 23 (east), go right on NY 22 (south) to NY 344, and turn left (east). Reach the HVRT parking area in 0.5 mile on the left.

This slightly dumbed-down version of the "East Street Shuffle" (Ride 26) is still a smart choice for a day when you don't have the time for a rubber-tired tour de force. This shorter route will show you the heavily forested area of the southern Taconic plateau north of Bash Bish Falls. You will be tempted by the endless backcountry roads between Great Barrington and Sheffield, Massachusetts, a good deal of them within easy reach of eastern Dutchess County. What a place to bring your bike and simply ride for a weekend.

The thing we like the most about this part of the Taconic region is the access to many bike routes and hiking trails that you can take right from the Taconic State Park public campground. A few times during the creation of this book, we camped for several days at a time at the park (and at Rudd Pond state campground to the south). This helped break up our research with rides on the Harlem Valley Rail Trail (which begins outside the campground entrance) and in the nearby Copake Hills. Although it may be a lifestyle quirk, we also find it easy and productive to do paperwork in a tent at a campsite, provided we avoid weekends, which can be pretty busy at this campground. For us, few things are more enjoyable than living and working out-of-doors. We use a large tent, in which we make room for a table and chairs. After a day's ride or hike, we also like to sleep in cots. If you approach camping this way, you'd be surprised at how much work you can get done, while relaxing at the same time. Watch your timing—busy weekends in any state campground will try your patience. In deference to campground management, lights out and quiet periods are rarely enforced.

0.00 Begin the tour from the HVRT parking lot, to the right immediately outside the campground. This is Bash Bish Falls Road, or NY 344. Bear left at the fork. Pass the Bash Bish parking area on your right, where a road also leads to a colony of rustic cottages, seasonally rented and owned by the state. Climb straight away.

You are ascending into the wildly scenic and romantic environs of Bash Bish Gorge; and you may, at certain times of year, be able to hear the falls from the road as you climb. (It is best visited from the Bash Bish parking areas on a footpath you'll see to the right.)

1.70 The hill tops out at the Bash Bish Falls State Park parking area (Mount Washington State Forest).

Welcome to Massachusetts! You follow through a long stretch of wilds. Wright Brook, the brook that leads to Bash Bish Falls, is on your right. Around 1845, John Frederick Kensett (1816–1872), a leading figure among the second-generation Hudson River School painters, was making preliminary field sketches for a series of five paintings of the falls, most notably his first Bash Bish Falls (1851). Other versions followed, leading to his 1855 masterwork by the same name.

3.20 Arrive at the intersection of Bash Bish Falls Road and West Street. There's a residence here and an old sign indicating Mount Everett. Bear right, cross the brook, and climb through the area known locally as Larch Hill. The road is lined, and there's a dirt shoulder. Traffic is light.

4.30 At a Y, bear right at Cross Street, remaining on West Street.

4.60 Cross City Brook and climb steadily but easily over dirt through the hardwoods.

5.00 West Street ends as it joins East Street. Go left. To the right about two hundred feet is the former Mount Washington State Forest headquarters. (See Ride 26 for more information.) Now you're on East Street, traveling north. This is a lined country road surrounded by woods. Pass a Nature Conservancy parcel on your right and descend.

6.20 Arrive at an intersection where Cross Road comes in from the left and Plantain Pond Road (dead end) departs to the right. Here you will see The Church of Christ Chapel, built in 1872; and behind it, the Mount Washington town hall. Continue straight ahead on East Street, trending downhill among the mountains and fields where views soon open up to the north. This is country cycling at its best!

9.40 Turn hard left onto West Street. Here the road is unlined and the surface is dirt.

9.70 Ignore a prominent left turn.

10.40 A sign announces that you are now on Sunset Road. You're crossing the state line, reentering New York now. A brisk descent of Dugway Hill begins. Be careful, for this is a one-lane, narrow road with a loose surface. As you cross the upper elevations of the Taconic ridge, note how the forest type turns briefly to mountain laurel and oak. You will pass a few trailheads that lead back to Taconic State Park here. The descent continues.

11.30 Pass the yellow snowmobile trail on the left.

12.00 Pass the blue trail and turn left onto North Mountain Road.

13.20 Turn left at the stop sign.

13.30 Turn left onto NY 344.

13.60 Arrive back at the HVRT parking area.

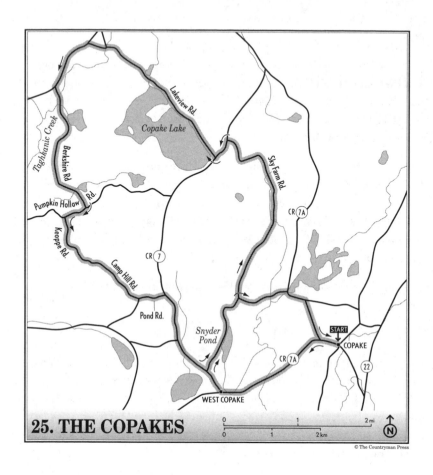

25. THE COPAKES

0   1   2 mi
0   1   2 km

Before the White Man:
The Copakes

DISTANCE: 18.1 miles

CUMULATIVE ELEVATION GAIN: 1031 feet

TERRAIN: Mildly hilly

DIFFICULTY: Moderate

RECOMMENDED BICYCLE: Mountain, hybrid

DIRECTIONS

From the intersection of NY 22 and CR 7A, bear west (left if you're coming north) onto CR 7A into the village of Copake (where the big clock sits in the middle of town). There's a general store where you can get lunch and snacks. Park anywhere. From the Taconic State Parkway, exit onto NY 23 (east), go right on NY 22 (south) to CR 7A.

There are so many beautiful back roads in eastern Columbia County that it seems a tragedy you can't ride them all. Well—theoretically—you could. The joy, of course, is in the fact that you can ride some of them, and from these experiences you can imagine future outings in new and unknown territory. This tour around the Copake Hills will have you covetously eyeing every little side road, farm lane, and byway; each one seeming more attractive than the last.

Begin in the tiny village of Copake (settled in 1755, established in 1824). There are many places to park. The easiest place to begin is from the town clock, which stands in the middle of the village. You are cordially invited by its owners, the Sood family, to park and begin your tour from the Copake General Store, where a luncheon barbecue is held on Saturdays and Sundays (weather permitting) during the summer. (For information call 518-329-4886.) You can also begin at Copake

Memorial Park on Mountain View Road, just north of the village off Farm Road.

0.00 Set to zero at the clock and head west on CR 7A, leaving the clock to your left.

0.30 CR 7A splits. Bear left. There's a double line and a bumpy shoulder here. Pass through open fields.

1.85 In West Copake, bear right on CR 7.

2.20 Turn right onto Snyder Pond Road. The street is unlined. Pass Snyder Pond on the right.

3.20 Break out into open fields as the scenery improves dramatically.

3.40 Turn left onto High Meadow Road. Over to your right (east) is the Taconic ridge, and the deep gash in the mountain where Bash Bish Falls lies hidden from view. There are sprawling cornfields and farms here.

4.50 Join Sky Farm Road, bearing left and climbing. (They don't call it Sky Farm Road for nothing.)

5.70 Pass Sky Top Road, a dead end to the left.

6.10 Turn left onto CR 7 and descend to Copake Lake.

6.40 Turn right onto Lakeview Road and follow along the edge of the lake, passing through a resortlike residential area with a few marinas and a golf course. Beyond the golf course you encounter pretty scenery once again, breaking out into high country. Lakeview Road becomes Copake Lake Road as it crosses the town line into Taghkanic. Come down a hill, cross the John Smith Bridge, and arrive at an intersection.

8.90 Go left on CR 11. There's a good shoulder here and the road is flat.

9.60 Turn left onto Berkshire Road. The road is not lined. Descend. Cross the Taghkanic Creek at the north end of Pumpkin Hollow Swamp.

The name comes from the Algonquian word meaning full of timber or water enough. There is a good deal of archaeological evidence supporting the fact that the Mohicans lived along this creek and in other areas of Copake from the Early to Late Woodlands Period. (The new, single residences that command large parcels of land are a prime example of how open space is rapidly being swallowed up here and in other highly desirable areas of the Hudson Valley.)

Now you pass through a far less appealing residential area, culminating with an Appalachian-looking game farm, and gleefully arrive at a T.

11.60 Turn right onto Pumpkin Hollow Road. Descend briefly.

11.90 Turn left onto Keoppe Road. This is a dirt single laner through the woods. *Before long you will see a WHEELCHAIR CROSSING sign, alerting you to the beginnings of Camp Hill Village. Everybody in this charming little farm community—a work and living place for mentally disabled adults—smiled and waved at us with great curiosity and enthusiasm. It seems to us one of the happiest communities we've encountered in a long time. The residents maintain a bakery that's open to the public.*

Keoppe Road changes into Camp Hill Road here. Continue through the Camp Hill community onto Pond Road (a.k.a. Chrysler Hill Road).

13.80 Turn right onto CR 7. There's no shoulder. Pass the West Copake Reformed Church. Descend.

14.60 Continue on CR 7 as CR 27 departs to the west. Descend.

15.10 Turn left onto Snyder Pond Road, which you'll recognize. This short backtrack will save you from doing more distance on CR 7, and the scenery is worth seeing twice.

16.40 Turn right onto High Meadow Road.
This road faithfully reflects its namesake with its dizzying array of dandelion and wildflower fields. Broad views stretch beyond little patches of hardwoods and white pines, and isolated, picturesque farms, furrowed cornfields, and timothy pastures dot the landscape. In the east, you see the deep and shadowed defile of Bash Bish lying folded and shadowed into the rumpled hills of the southern Taconic plateau. Views like these, together with the following descent and a warm summer breeze, is what backroad biking is all about!

17.1 Pass Robinson Pond Dam on your left and continue on this section of lined, soft-shouldered road (CR 7A), passing Langdonhurst Market where they sell farm goods and—you are in such luck—homemade ice cream.

18.00 Turn left at the Y where CR 7A comes together, and ride 0.3 miles back to the clock.

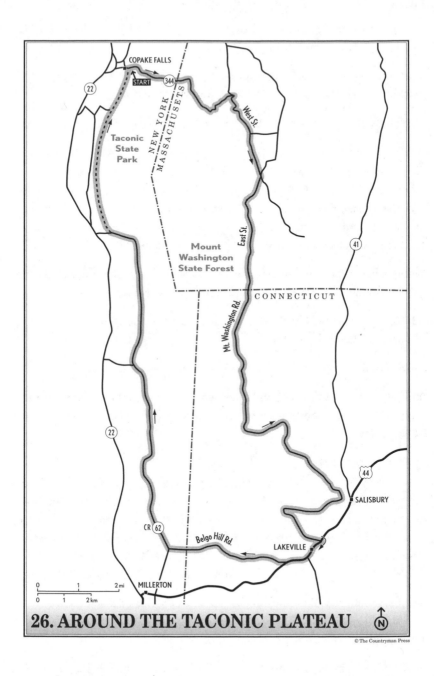

COPAKE FALLS

22

START

344

West St.

NEW YORK
MASSACHUSETS

Taconic
State
Park

Mount
Washington
State Forest

East St.

41

Mt. Washington Rd.

CONNECTICUT

22

44

SALISBURY

CR 62

Belgo Hill Rd.

LAKEVILLE

0   1   2 mi
0   1   2 km

MILLERTON

26. AROUND THE TACONIC PLATEAU

N

© The Countryman Press

The East Street Shuffle: Around the Taconic Plateau

DISTANCE: 33.5 miles

CUMULATIVE ELEVATION GAIN: 3800 feet

TERRAIN: Hilly

DIFFICULTY: Strenuous

RECOMMENDED BICYCLE: Mountain, hybrid (long dirt sections)

DIRECTIONS

From the intersection of NY 22 and NY 344 in Copake Falls, New York, turn east (right, if you're coming north) onto NY 344 and go 0.5 mile to the Harlem Valley Rail Trail (HVRT). Park on the left in the HVRT parking lot on CR 344 (a.k.a. Bash Bish Falls Road), opposite the Depot Deli, between the bike shop and the Taconic State Park campground entrance. Information, maps, and last-minute provisions can be had here.

The Taconic Mountains are a relatively low, elongated plateau of hills stretching from southwestern Vermont and Massachusetts and into western Connecticut and New York. The ridge is very popular with hikers, who walk the extensive southern Taconic trail network, and with cyclists, who pedal the northern section of the Harlem Valley Rail Trail (HVRT) and the back roads of eastern Columbia County. However, the backcountry beyond the rail trail to the east of the ridge remains an undiscovered jewel for those interested in longer trips over widely varied terrain, some of it surprisingly isolated. The ride can be easily broken up into an exciting overnight, if you're willing to carry a tent. Although the area is lightly inhabited, the sense of wilderness is profound. This ride ranks with "The Holy Grail" (Ride 13) in distance and difficulty, except that you can get food in Lakeville or Millerton about halfway through the trip and hole up in a B&B if you want. Be flawlessly prepared for any emergency. The first store you will encounter is over 18 miles from the start. There's a bike shop in Millerton.

0.00 Head left out of the parking lot (east) on NY 344, passing the Bash Bish parking area (take a look at the kiosk map) to your right.

The falls themselves are only visible from below, along a foot trail beginning at the parking area. The 1.5-mile round-trip walk to the falls can be taken later, from the HVRT parking lot, if you find yourself with the energy and the time—but by all means try to see the falls.

Set out! Immediately a steep ascent takes you along the deep ravine on your right.

1.70 The climb tops out at the Bash Bish parking area. A sign indicates that this is Mount Washington State Forest in Massachusetts. Don't bother with trying to find the obscured view from Eagle's Nest—it's not worth your time. Now you go downhill next to Bash Bish Brook. The road is paved.

3.20 Reach the intersection of NY 344 and West Street.

A delightfully weather-beaten, antique iron sign says MOUNT EVERETT, but you can't read the rest. The Appalachian Trail (AT) summits Mount Everett about 3 miles to the east. Turn right here, cross Wright Brook, and granny your way up a short, steep hill. This is Larch Hill, named for the appearance of the deciduous conifers you'll see along the road. The residences are few and in good taste.

3.90 Breaking out of the climb, you descend, remaining on West Street. The surface turns to dirt.

4.30 Bear right at a triangle, leaving Cross Road to your left.

4.60 Cross City Brook and climb steadily but easily over dirt through the hardwoods.

5.20 West Street ends as it joins East Street. Bear right, and you'll arrive at the Mount Washington State Forest headquarters (across from the YMCA camp entrance).

This is no longer the official headquarters and is not staffed except by maintenance personnel. Primitive campsites are available 1.5 miles from the road in the vicinity of Ashley

Hill Brook. (If you're headed that way, we strongly advise the use of the Ashley Brook Trail to the Blue Trail, instead of using the Alander Mountain Trail.) Maps are available at the trailhead kiosk. The trails are multi-use designated.

Continue along East Street through deep woods on dirt. Wetlands appear east of the road on private property. You're entering a long stretch of forest now.

8.20 Pass the (unsigned) Mount Frissell Trailhead, marked by red discs. This is the Massachusetts and Connecticut state line. East Street becomes Mount Washington Road now.

Three hundred feet ahead, at the Appalachian Mountain Club parking area, a foot trail goes to Sage's Ravine (on the AT) and points north and south. Camping is permitted in designated sites off the road.

8.50 Pass the Bear Mountain Trailhead, which crosses the private Mount Riga Preserve (public access permitted, no camping).

11.50 Pass South Lake. To the right, take a look at the Riga blast furnace (the last such furnace standing in Connecticut) and descend through the bucolic Wachocasttinook ravine. The drop is steep and the surface is loose and rocky in spots—all of it dirt or sandy loam—so be careful.

14.00 Pass through a gate as pavement begins. Go through a pair of stop signs.

14.50 Bear right and descend on Bunker Hill Road (light traffic, no shoulder, 25 mph).

15.00 Go right onto Selleck Hill Road and pump your way uphill.

The scenery—and the homesteads—are extraordinary. This is farm country. Open views of the Taconics and the surrounding hills and pastures are sensational. If you can ignore such an endorsement, it should be noted that if pressed you could avoid this hill, shaving off 2.8 miles by continuing downhill on Bunker Hill Road to US 44, but traffic can be fast and busy so we don't recommend it.

Note: US 44, which spans New York and Connecticut, is signed as CT 44 and NY 44 out on the highways themselves.

16.50 Bear left and descend on Lincoln City Road (dirt).

17.20 The road turns to pavement.

17.80 Bear right on US 44 and go downhill. You can ride either the sidewalk or the wide shoulder. This is a speed zone.

18.30 Pull into Lakeville, Connecticut.

Here you can reprovision. Although not much in the way of services is immediately apparent, there is a service station, and a pizza place and café on Ethan Allen Street off Holley Street. Go through the light at the intersection of CR 41, remaining on US 44, and take a left on Holley Street. (Or, stay on CR 41 and take the first right.) Here stood the famous Holley Manufacturing Company (1844). It was built on the site of a 1762 blast furnace that was a leading arsenal in the Revolutionary War. Across the street, a picnic table appears to the right at the edge of a pond, and if you're so inclined, you can swim in Lake Wononscopomuc (small fee) at the Salisbury Town Grove, which you'll see just beyond. There's no real sense of a village here; and at the risk of offending the good citizens of Lakeville, we have to admit that nearby Salisbury, a mile or so east on US 44, commands a good deal more charm and tourist appeal. There again, you're committed to riding along US 44.

As you climb easily out of Lakeville on a wide shoulder along US 44, watch on your right for Belgo Hill Road, which appears just before the speed zone intensifies from 25 to 40 mph.

18.80 Turn right and climb on Belgo Hill Road (no shoulder or lines). Continue straight through the next intersection. After a brief climb, the road descends long and winding through open pastures. Belgo Hill Road becomes Shagroy Road as you descend into New York State, where the road quality deteriorates markedly.

21.70 Arrive at CR 62 and go right (north).

Note that the pretty, interesting village of Millerton (the home of Village Bicycle Shop on South Center Street and the trailhead of the Millerton-Wassaic section of the HVRT) lies only a mile-plus to the south on CR 62 to US 44. Millerton is much larger (and more interesting) than Lakeville, with many more services to chose from, and there's a great diner at the HVRT intersection.

CR 62 is a mellow road, but for much of its distance it lacks a solid shoulder. In 1 mile you pass Rudd Pond, where there's a state campground. Continue along CR 62, straight through the intersection where it becomes CR 63 (Boston Corners Road).

27.80 Go through Boston Corners, a four-way intersection.

The world's first legal heavyweight prizefight was held here. The road (now called Under Mountain Road) is at one point tunneled over in old sugar maples, and far-reaching views across the Harlem Valley and the Taconic uplands encompass farms, corn and buckwheat fields, horse pastures, and seemingly endless hills.

29.30 Turn right onto the rail trail (HVRT).

This level stretch of paved trail through the woods will take you back to the HVRT trailhead and parking area where you began (with one turn onto Valley View Road where you go right for 0.4 mile to pick up the rail trail again on the left).

33.50 Arrive at the HVRT parking area.

For more information about cycling in rural areas east of the Taconics, consult Andi Marie Cantele's *Backroad Bicycling in Western Massachusetts.*

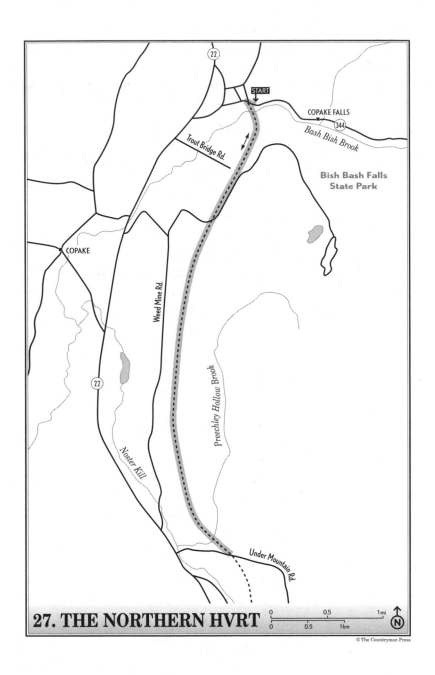

22

START

COPAKE FALLS

344

Bash Bish Brook

Trout Bridge Rd.

**Bish Bash Falls
State Park**

COPAKE

Weed Mine Rd.

Preechley Hollow Brook

22

Noster Kill

Under Mountain Rd.

27. THE NORTHERN HVRT

0   0.5   1mi
0   0.5   1km

N

Foggy Mountain Breakdown: The Northern HVRT

DISTANCE: 7.8 miles

CUMULATIVE ELEVATION GAIN: 400 feet

TERRAIN: Slight grade

DIFFICULTY: Easy

RECOMMENDED BICYCLE: Mountain, hybrid, road

DIRECTIONS

From the intersection of NY 22 and NY 344 in Copake Falls, New York, turn east (right, if you're coming north) onto NY 344 and go 0.5 miles to the Harlem Valley Rail Trail (HVRT). Park on the left in the HVRT parking lot. From the Taconic State Parkway, exit onto NY 23 (east), go right on NY 22 (south) to NY 344, and turn left (east). Reach the HVRT parking area in 0.5 mile on the left.

This is a short tour that begins at the Harlem Valley Rail Trail (HVRT) parking area in Copake Falls, next to the Taconic State Park campground. Combined with the hiking trails and mountain bike routes in the area, there's a lot here to make for a fun family weekend. There's a short walk to the nearby Bash Bish Falls and a great swimming hole (Ore Pit Pond) at the campground. This little tour is highly recommended to those with small children or tag-a-longs, or for riders who want to take a break from the longer tours on the nearby county roads that are described in this book.

This paved section of the HVRT runs from the Taconic State Park Recreation Area in the north (the area including the trails, campground, and Bash Bish Falls) to Weed Mines on Under Mountain Road, 4 miles to the south. The area is rural, and the trail is very popular with local cyclists and walkers, especially on nice weekends during the summer and fall. So, although the route is remote, you will probably have enough company so that it does not seem isolated. There are no stores or services along the way. Stock up on goodies at the Depot Deli, right at the trailhead. There's also a bike shop here. Head south on the paved rail trail.

0.00 From the Harlem Valley Rail Trail parking area, head south. (It's the only way you can go at this writing; the railbed to the north is unimproved.)

0.60 Join Valley View Road (paved), which follows the route of the original railbed for a short distance. (This is the only section of road you'll have to deal with.) Take a left onto the HVRT.

Now you ride along through the woods under the Taconic plateau that you see to your left. You're looking up at Alander, Bash Bish, and the Washburn mountains. There are several tractor crossings that may be in use. The trail is about 10 feet wide, and there are benches spread out along the way amid the open fields of timothy and alfalfa.

3.90 The end. Turn around and retrace your steps back to the trailhead parking area.

The New York and Harlem Railroad opened in 1832 and at first used horse-drawn cars. By 1852, it extended north to Chatham, with a total of 130 miles of track. Passenger service was discontinued in 1972. The HVRT will run from Wassaic to Chatham, New York, when completed. The right-of-way north of Copake is at this time privately owned. The Harlem Valley Rail Trail Association encourages memberships that support their volunteer trail maintenance program and acquisition efforts. For information, go to www.hvrt.org.

7.80 Arrive back at the HVRT parking area.

Dutchess County

28

Tivoli and Clermont State Historic Site

DISTANCE: 16.5 miles

CUMULATIVE ELEVATION GAIN: 425 feet

TERRAIN: Hilly

DIFFICULTY: Easy

RECOMMENDED BICYCLE: Mountain, hybrid, road

DIRECTIONS

From the large intersection of NY 9G and NY 199, 3 miles east of the Kingston-Rhinecliff Bridge toll plaza on the border of the Rhinebeck and Red Hook village limits, set to zero and go north on NY 9G. In 3.5 miles, pass the entrance to Bard College on the left. At 6 miles watch carefully for CR 78. Take this left, heading west into town. Go through the intersection of Broadway, North Road, and Montgomery Street, and turn right within a half block into the municipal parking area.

The little village of Tivoli is a collage of oldness, newness, youth, establishment, and antiquity. It is shabby chic and tattooed but never

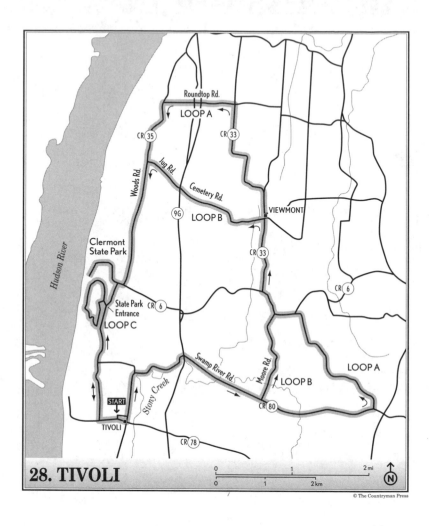

Roundtop Rd.

LOOP A

CR 35   CR 33

Jug Rd.

Woods Rd.

Cemetery Rd.

9G   LOOP B   VIEWMONT

Hudson River

Clermont
State Park

CR 33

CR 6

State Park
Entrance   CR 6

LOOP C

Swamp River Rd.   Moore Rd.   LOOP A

LOOP B

Stony Creek

CR 80

START

TIVOLI

CR 78

28. TIVOLI

0   1   2 mi
0   1   2 km

N

© The Countryman Press

grunge; it is elegant and old-monied yet unpretentious. It's a colorful
college berg, a restive river town; and, with its interesting, offbeat little
shops and eateries, it's just a plain nice place to visit. Clermont (Livingston Manor, 1730), the historic estate of Chancellor Livingston, is close
by, joined to Tivoli by lazy thoroughfares through the sleepy outskirts
of town. Through this matrix of scenic back roads traversing open farm
country and dense woods, the boisterous Roelff-Jansen Kill winds its
way over, under, and down to dissolution with the Hudson, as if to tie
your experience up in a neat, sylvan knot.

Clermont, Robert Livingston's birthplace

Because the lands next to the Hudson River provided easy transportation and were among the first to be privately purchased and developed, there's not much in the way of public riverside road mileage on
either side of the river today. But in the quiet lands above the river,
and in the hinterlands beyond the great colonial estates forged out of
the early Dutch patroonships, there are endless miles of gently rolling-
to-flat terrain, spotted with rambling horse pastures, gridded with orchards and hillside farms, and rife with fecund wheat fields, tangled
briar patches, and juniper thickets.

As if from a Hudson River School landscape, this ride features dark,
backdrop swamps of standing dead hardwood where the deer come to
drink. These are the gem roads you only dream of cycling on—and
which you would normally miss as you travel north and south on
NY 9 and NY 9G—the paved colonial routes that carried armies and

commerce between New York and Albany, past tiny agrarian settlements with place names like Bingham Mills, Buckwheat Bridge, and Cedar Hill.

Get organized in the municipal parking lot. There's a very good Mexican restaurant (Santa Fe) on the corner and an antiquarian bookstore nearby where you can buy a county road map. There's Tivoli Bread and Baking, with good coffee, scones, lemon squares, and more just down the street. There's a corner store, a sushi bar, a town hall with a visitors center, and so on. Indulge yourself. You're about to work some of it off, anyway.

LOOP A

0.00 Come out of the lot and turn left. Go a half block, to the intersection of North Road, Montgomery Street, and Broadway. Turn left onto North Road, a quiet, residential street. Bear right at the first intersection, leaving Sengstack Road and a big horse farm to your left.

0.80 Pass a brisk little falls (seasonal) on the right, tumbling over a low dam on Stony Creek (a.k.a. Swamp River). Open fields and woods follow.

1.50 Arrive at the corner of NY 9G and Stony Brook Road and carefully go across NY 9G onto CR 80 (a.k.a. Lasher Road, Swamp River Road). This is a double-lined road at this point, with a fog line and a grassy, cinder shoulder, that heads east through a semi-residential, semirural area.

2.70 Pass Moore Road on the left.

3.60 Enter Columbia County. The road becomes CR 4.

4.00 A large hillside orchard appears on the right. Watch for a turn on the left.

4.30 Turn left onto Nevis Road. The road is unlined. There are big views of the Catskills on your left, to the west.

6.20 Merge with CR 6 and bear left. This is a lined road, with a fog line obscured by gravel. You look west, straight toward Overlook Mountain in the Catskills as you ride.

6.50 Pass Moores Road on the left.

6.70 Go right onto CR 33. There's a vineyard on the right. The terrain is gently rolling. This road is lined. Traffic is sparse. There are woodlands, red barns, silos, fields, and views to the west here.

7.80 Pass Cemetery Road, then the Lutheran Church. Welcome to Viewmont (no services).

9.55 Turn left onto Roundtop Road.

Perhaps this road is named for the views of Roundtop Mountain in the Catskills (at one time thought to be the Catskills' highest peak) or for the nearby local hills, Roundtop and Little Roundtop.

Be careful as you approach NY 9G. Cross NY 9G, continuing straight on Roundtop Road. Go straight through another little intersection with East Camp Road, named for the Palatine settlement.

10.50 Turn left on Woods Road, CR 35. This is a lined road. This is perhaps the prettiest road on the route. Climb for a while. The road soon levels out.

11.40 Pass Jug Road on the left.

12.40 Pass Clermont Farms. This is a large and covetable horse farm. The traffic is mellow. There's a fog line, a shoulder, and big white pines and maples. Pass the Carmelite Sisters Convent.

13.00 At the corner of CR 6, leave CR 35. Bear right, then bear left.

13.50 Pass the Clermont State Historic Site maintenance center on your left and turn right off Woods Road into Clermont's main entrance.

Whatever you do, don't miss this short side trip. There's a booth where grounds fees are collected. It's your lucky day because there's no charge for bikes. Glide down the beautifully wooded driveway. You'll see the mansion and a parking area and picnic grounds to your left, with a rest room. The views of the Catskill Escarpment across the river are expansive. You're right on the river now. In season, the gardens and house can be toured.

The site is preserved to its 1930 appearance. Seven successive generations of the Livingston family lived here at Robert Livingston's birthplace. You can read about Chancellor Livingston on a historic plaque. He did a lot. He was, among other things, a member of Congress, Chancellor of New York, Minister to France, Secretary of Foreign Affairs, negotiator of the Louisiana Purchase, and committee member of the five original drafters of the Declaration of Independence. He administered the oath to George Washington as first president of the United States and shared with Robert Fulton in the invention of the steamboat (he gave money). There are rest rooms on site and a very well-appointed visitor center (free).

You can see the Saugerties lighthouse from here (now a B&B), out across the river and slightly south. You see several peaks in the Indian Head Wilderness Area to the west.

14.40 Return to Woods Road from your visit to Clermont. Turn right, and continue on CR 6 (Woods Road), immediately entering Dutchess County. There are no lines on the road.

16.20 Turn left onto Broadway in Tivoli and pedal back to the parking lot.

16.50 Arrive at the parking lot.

LOOP B (SHORTENED VERSION OF MAIN ROUTE; 12.6 MILES)

0.00 At the intersection of North Road and Broadway, turn left onto North Road.

0.80 Pass the waterfall.

1.50 Cross NY 9G onto CR 80.

2.70 Turn left onto scenic Moores Road.

2.90 Cross a creek.

4.00 Turn left onto CR 6.

4.30 Turn right onto CR 33. Vineyards on right.

5.00 Enter Viewmont. Turn left onto unlined Cemetery Road and head west.

6.70 At the corner of Cemetery Road, Jug Road, and NY 9G, go across NY 9G onto Jug Road.

7.20 Arrive at CR 35. Turn left.

9.00 Turn right onto CR 6.

9.40 Turn right into Clermont State Park, go down to the river and picnic area, and return to CR 6.

10.80 Turn right onto CR 6 (Woods Road).

12.30 Turn left on Broadway and ride into Tivoli.

12.60 Arrive at the parking lot.

LOOP C (TIVOLI TO CLERMONT STATE HISTORIC SITE; 5 MILES)

0.00 Turn right (west) out of the Tivoli municipal parking lot.

0.30 Turn right (north) onto Woods Road, CR 6.

1.90 Turn left into the Clermont State Historic Site and go down to the river, then return to CR 6.

3.00 Turn right onto CR 6.

4.70 Turn left onto Broadway.

5.00 Arrive at the parking lot.

29

Snoopy and the Red Baron: Red Hook

DISTANCE: Loop A, 12.5 miles; Loop B, 16 miles

CUMULATIVE ELEVATION GAIN: Loop A, 630 feet; Loop B, 850 feet

TERRAIN: Both loops are moderately hilly

DIFFICULTY: Loop A, moderate; Loop B, strenuous

RECOMMENDED BICYCLE: Mountain, hybrid, road (touring bikes are best suited to Loop B)

DIRECTIONS

From NY 199 and NY 9G, 1.5 miles east of the Kingston-Rhinecliff Bridge, set to zero and go north on NY 9G. At 1.9 miles, turn right onto NY 199, toward the town of Red Hook. At 3.6 miles, you're at the intersection of US 9 and NY 199 (East/West Market Street). The tour mileage begins from this intersection. You can park anywhere in town, but the most convenient is the municipal lot shared by the CVS parking lot, a few hundred feet north on US 9 (North Broadway).

LOOP A (MOSTLY COUNTRY AND WOODS ROADS)

0.00 Orient yourself on East Market Street (NY 199 east), in the heart of town, and ride cautiously along the road or walk the sidewalk until you can cycle comfortably through this fairly congested area. Make your way east along the shoulder.

0.80 Turn right onto Orlich Road and immediately bear right onto Norton Road. This will take you through a dull residential area for a short distance. Soon

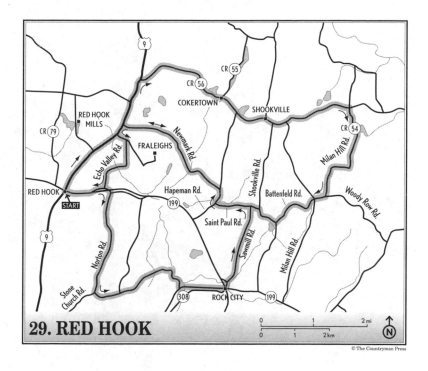

29. RED HOOK

© The Countryman Press

you're passing little juniper thickets on an unlined, lightly trafficked back road, where deer stand in people's driveways. The road becomes more rural.

2.70 Pass the Old Rhinebeck Aerodrome and bear left onto Stone Church Road.

By all means treat yourself to a World War I–style air show if you have the time. On sunny days in the summer, you will see the biplanes circling overhead, dogfighting, and maybe even barnstorming. (It wasn't really Snoopy, but an Englishman, who shot down the Red Baron.) This is a lined road but only for a short distance. You can take some comfort in knowing that most of the stunt drivers in town are aloft. Climb now.

Stone Church Road becomes Oriole Mills Road as it enters the town of Milan.

3.40 Pass Pells Road. Now you're in pure woods on a dirt road. This may be one of the places where your skinny tires just don't do. A cross bike would be perfect for this terrain, or a hybrid/mountain bike. You go past a summer camp at the point where there's a creek; and as you continue, a pretty little millpond and farmstead.

A cyclist enjoys the wide shoulders of NY 308.

4.60 At the corner of Oriole Mills Road and Old Rock City Road, turn left at Maple Shade Farm and continue through an area of extensive woodlots and old homes. The road is not lined.

4.90 Be alert as you merge with NY 308 (Rock City Road) and go left. There's a nice, wide shoulder.

5.40 At the end of NY 308, where it merges with NY 199, you're at the crossing known as Rock City. Your destination is Rock City Road, which is across NY 199 to your left (north). Use caution as you cross. There's a light here, but traffic on NY 199 can be heedless.

Cross onto Rock City Road and bear right immediately onto Sawmill Road at 5.5 miles. Go uphill gently and steadily for about 1 mile. The houses are interesting through here.

6.50 Crest the hill and descend lazily.

7.00 Turn left onto Saint Paul Road, an area of interesting-looking houses and nice woods. Descend a bit. The road changes to Shookville Road as you reenter Red Hook Township.

7.60 Turn right onto Hapeman Road at the site of a red barn at Cherry Hill Farm. *The road is unlined, with little or no shoulder.*

7.90 Go left onto Feller Newmark Road and climb briefly. Now you have a long glide to look forward to. Be careful; even though these little roads are self-limiting speed-wise, people still hog the centerline.

8.90 Pass Crestwood Road, the site of a gorgeous little farm. This looks like the lesser taken of two roads and may therefore appear more attractive, but it soon loses its appeal as it passes through a new residential area. Continue on Feller Newmark Road. This is the historic hamlet of Fraleighs.

9.40 Some scant views of the Catskills appear. *You're looking right at Overlook and the broad, flat lower promontory known as Minister's Face. Indian Head lies in the north.*

10.00 Go through an orchard area with good scenery.

10.20 This is US 9 (a.k.a. Albany-Post Road). Turn left and stay right on the shoulder. This is a sanctioned bike route, so drivers are at least aware that it's a shared roadway. You're on it for a very short distance.

10.40 Turn left onto Fraleigh Lane.

10.60 Turn right onto Echo Valley Road.

11.20 At a quaint farmstead cross the Saw Kill. The neighborhood loses its character as you approach town. The architecture becomes plain; the development is an imposition.

11.80 At the corner of Echo Valley Road and NY 199, turn right and ride back toward town on a good shoulder.

12.50 Red Hook village.

LOOP B (MOSTLY COUNTY ROADS)

This is a longer tour, which focuses more on the ride than the countryside, but gives you a good dose of both. Begin at the main intersection of Red Hook, where Loop A begins, and head north on US 9. There's a good shoulder on this sanctioned, state bike route, which is called the Hudson River Greenway Trail and signed as a shared roadway. It is a popular route with serious cyclists who are comfortable with the conditions of a large, shared roadway. Traffic can be fast, but the shoulder is wide. Personally, we don't enjoy spending too much time on shared roadways, especially when there are so many one laners around. But the mileage on US 9 is minimal—then you cut east into the less-used county roads of Upper Red Hook and Cokertown.

0.00 Leave Red Hook and go north on US 9.

2.50 Turn right onto CR 56 (Old Spring Lake Road). The road is lined. There's not much of a shoulder.

4.20 Bear right, remaining on CR 56, as it becomes Cokertown Road. Avoid bearing left on the continuation of Old Spring Lake Road.

5.40 Pass Shookville on the right.

6.90 At the corner of CR 54 (Milan Hill Road), go right.

8.00 Pass an old abandoned farm at the junction of Willow Glen Road.

9.00 Pass Woody Road on the left.

9.20 Turn right onto Becker Hill Road.

9.25 Go left onto Battenfeld Road.

10.20 Turn right onto Shookville Road. Turn left onto Saint Paul Road. Join Loop A at the intersection of Sawmill and Saint Paul roads. (See mile 7 on Loop A for return directions.)

16.00 Arrive in Red Hook village.

Why not add some excitement to your ride with a barnstorming flight in a 1929 New Standard, open cockpit biplane? The Old Rhinebeck Aerodrome museum is open daily mid-May through October. Airshows are conducted every Saturday and Sunday from mid-June through mid-October, beginning at 2 PM. For information, go to www.old rhinebeck.org.

30

The Miller's Tale: Millerton

DISTANCE: 18.5 miles

CUMULATIVE ELEVATION GAIN: 1843 feet

TERRAIN: Hilly

DIFFICULTY: Moderate

RECOMMENDED BICYCLE: Mountain, hybrid, road

DIRECTIONS

Millerton, New York, is located at the intersections of NY 22 and NY 44 in northeastern Dutchess County, near the Columbia County border. Park in the municipal lot on Main Street in Millerton just east of NY 22, where you'll see the trailhead for Harlem Valley Rail Trail (HVRT).

This ride was recommended to us by Mike Anelli, owner of Village Bicycles in the village of Millerton, Northeast Township (incorporated 1875). As the owner of a bike shop, you'd expect a guy like Mike to be a serious rider—and he is—a fit and strong cycling enthusiast. Accordingly, this tends to be a ride for the more serious rider, not because it's long, but because it covers a good deal of its mileage on hilly county roads. Mike put it like this: "The county roads around here are great riding because there's so little traffic and the scenery is unbelievable. I tend to just take off on numbered roads that I know, and then I expand from there, pushing into new territory. This is one place where I like to do that." He drew his thumb across the area west of Millerton in Northeast and Ancram townships (Dutchess and Columbia counties) and roughed out the route that you see here. Only about half of the

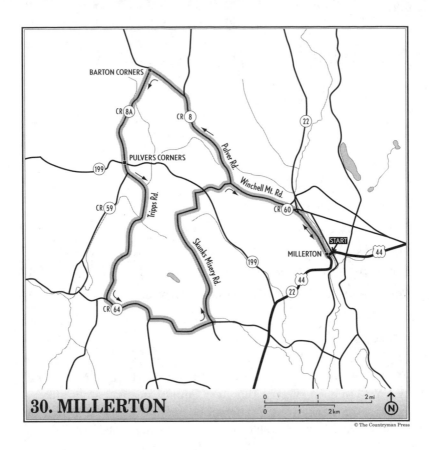

30. MILLERTON

© The Countryman Press

tour uses county roads (which have light traffic), and the other half is on unlined, backcountry byways and one laners.

0.00 From the Harlem Valley Rail Trail (HVRT) parking area in Millerton, turn right onto US 44 and right again at the light onto NY 22. This short section of highway isn't the greatest, surface or traffic-wise, but it's a short section, most of it contained in a 30 mph speed zone.

0.70 Bear left onto Winchell Mountain Road (CR 60) and climb ravenously. The scenery becomes dramatic as the road levels out into open country.

2.40 Turn right onto Stan Pulver Road (a.k.a. Pulver Road, CR 8) and ride past a large farm through open fields. The road flattens and then descends. You're up high, looking northwest across Ancram and Gallatin Townships. Coming down a long hill, leave East Ancram Road to your right. The shoulder is very limited, but there's plenty of sight distance on this road and not much traffic (as promised).

5.10 At Barton Corners, turn left onto CR 8A. This is the same kind of road as CR 8—lined, a soft shoulder, and a pastoral setting. It's even less busy. Ascend.

6.40 Enter Dutchess County, where CR 8A becomes Bean River Road. There's no ridable shoulder—just room to bail out if need be.

7.00 Cross NY 199 at Pulvers Corners onto CR 59.

7.20 Take the first left off CR 59 onto Tripps Road. This is more like it—a road that you pretty much have to yourself. There's no line or shoulder. Just black tar and big working farms. Horses and cows gawk at you and farmers wave.

10.00 Turn left onto CR 64 (North East Center Road) and climb McGee Hill.

11.50 Descend gratefully. There are miles of scenery and long white fences here. Centerlines, fog lines, soft shoulders, and mellow traffic greet you.

12.50 Right in the middle of a screaming downhill, make a near 180-degree left turn onto Skunks Misery Road, and as you may have suspected, climb. This is an unlined, heavily wooded back road. Pass a small pond.

14.50 Top out and begin descending.

14.90 Pass Brigadoon Farm.

This place is fully in command of the surrounding valley and reminiscent of the sentimental play; but take heed to beware the Brigadoon killer cow, noting how each tine of his massive horns would fit neatly between your nice new Spinergy wheels. As if in the setting of a picturesque drama, you can see the road stretching out for miles ahead of you. Follow it.

15.50 Bear left on NY 199 and immediately turn right onto Winchell Mountain Road (CR 60). Climb (again). Actually, the shoulder's not bad on this section.

16.20 Pulver Road departs to the left (northwest). Now you know the way home. Descend on Winchell Mountain Road.

17.90 Arrive at NY 22 and carefully merge right.

18.50 Arrive in Millerton and bear left onto US 44 to the HVRT parking lot.
Take a moment to say "Hi" to Mike at the bike shop, where you might like to try lifting a carbon fiber bike frame with your pinkie. If you've got the energy, you can ride the HVRT to the south as far as Wassaic and back up again, or north to the Copake Falls area, where the northern terminus of the HVRT ends near Bash Bish Falls. Ask Mike about other, longer road rides, both on the New York side and the Connecticut and Massachusetts side—for they are endless.

31

In the Land of Tishasink: Pine Plains

DISTANCE: 22.9 miles

CUMULATIVE ELEVATION CHANGE: 1700 feet

TERRAIN: Hills

DIFFICULTY: Strenuous

RECOMMENDED BICYCLE: Mountain, hybrid, road (some dirt sections)

DIRECTIONS

To reach Pine Plains from the Taconic State Parkway, take Exit 44 to NY 82 north. At the corner of NY 199 and NY 82 and CR 83A, the main intersection in Pine Plains, go north a half block on CR 83A (North Main Street) and park in the municipal lot behind the Stissing National Bank.

The far-fetched views and farmsteads of northeast Dutchess have a rough-hewn and pleasing frontier appearance, compared to the manicured estates and sprawling horse farms of the southeastern county—and with this rough edge comes a bewitching, wild charm. Barns tucked into stony, brambly hillsides, islands of elegant hardwood in open fields of sculpted furrows, impenetrable hedgerows of briar thickets and scarlet barberry; this is a world of ancient farms and oceanic fields, wrenched from the grip of nature by generations of tough Palatine settlers. It was apparently a hard life, but by most accounts, a good one. And what we see today are the pleasing results of that relentless toil—all 250 years of a seasoned and fruitful landscape that began with a Moravian Mission around 1740.

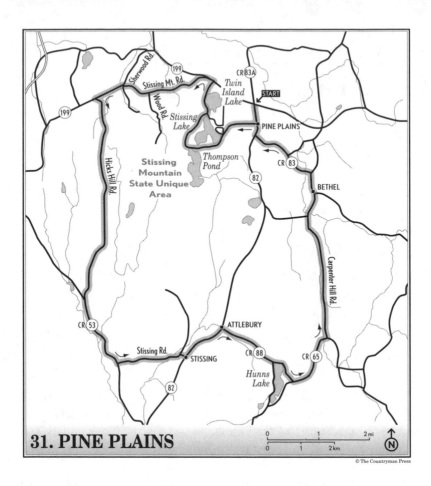

31. PINE PLAINS

© The Countryman Press

The old farm and forest roads of Pine Plains fit neatly into a strenuous 20-plus miler that will take you all the way around Stissing Mountain, up and down hills and across ridges, over creeks and through orchards, along dirt single laners, and on a few mellow county highways. Come prepared to spend the day, carry your tools, bring plenty of water and snacks, and pack a few layers. These are not flat miles, so the trip seems a little longer than an average 20-mile tour.

0.00 Head south on NY 82 through a pretty residential section.

0.40 Turn right onto Lake Road.

Directly ahead you'll see the Stissing Ridge. Stissing, with its tower, is on the south end of the ridge. Stissing is named for Tishasink (folk-typonomized to Stissing), a Mahican chief who lived in the notch between Stissing and Little Stissing Mountain.

1.20 Ride along the edge of Stissing Lake. This is fast becoming a built-up residential area.

You'll see signs here for the Thompson Pond Nature Preserve, which is at the edge of Thompson Pond. This 500-acre nature conservancy preserve is a national natural landmark, an excellent example of a calcareous wetland. Thompson Pond is a kettle hole, formed 15 thousand years ago when pebbles and gravel from melting streams settled on glacial ice and then collapsed to form this steep-sided pond during the Pleistocene epoch.

This is considered the best birding spot in the Hudson Valley, aside from the Hudson River itself. It's considered the best place in the state to see golden eagles. We took that with a grain of salt, but on our first visit to the preserve in early April, we got very close to a recently migrated nesting pair. They are larger than bald eagles, with a wingspan to 6 feet. Habitat degradation has taken its toll on these birds (You see those nice new houses all around?), causing infant mortality rates over 75 percent. No bikes are allowed on preserve lands, but stop to take a look along the roadside.

2.10 On the left is the blue-marked trail to Stissing summit.

2.80 Beach Road appears on the right. Continue straight ahead. Ride along the edge of Twin Island Lake.

3.50 Turn left onto NY 199. This is a busy road, but you're not on it for long. Stay right. There's a decent shoulder.

3.70 Turn left onto Stissing Mountain Road. There are no lines or shoulders here. Climb.

4.30 You can see Stissing on your left as you climb into an area of high, exposed pastures. Ahead you will see the Catskill mountains. That's Kaaterskill High Peak on the right.

4.90 Glide downhill past Wood Road.

5.40 Bear right at Sherwood Road and turn left on NY 199. Be careful. The shoulder is marginal, and traffic is faster here.

6.10 Turn left on Hicks Hill Road. Climb. You'll have open views of the Stissing Ridge on the left.

9.50 A long downhill brings you past the westerly bounds of the Stissing multi-use area.

10.10 Turn left on CR 53 (Cold Spring Road). The shoulder is broken tar and cinder. The traffic is sparse in comparison to NY 199. Use caution. Motorists may not be accustomed to seeing many bicycles in this area.

11.70 Turn left onto Stissing Road and pass several quaint colonial homesteads.

12.90 Turn right onto Stissing Lane. (You can't shortcut left; it's a dead end.)

13.20 Turn left onto NY 82. There's a narrow but workable shoulder. Now, Stissing Mountain is on your left as you ride north.

14.40 Turn right onto CR 88 (Attlebury Hill Road) and climb. If you've had enough at this point, you can judge the traffic on NY 82 and take it back to Pine Plains if you prefer to avoid the hills ahead.

15.50 Merge onto CR 65, bearing left on Hunns Lake Road, passing Hunns Lake on the right.

16.20 Bear left, remaining on CR 65.

17.40 Turn left on Carpenter Hill Road, which is unlined with no shoulder.

18.20 Pass Conklin Hill Road.

18.70 Begin a long descent.

19.90 At the intersection of Carpenter Hill and Bethel Cross Road, cross the Shekomeko Creek. At Bethel, an early farm crossing, turn left onto CR 83. Pass CR 70 and come downhill.

22.20 Turn right on NY 82 (north) and head back into Pine Plains.

22.90 Arrive in Pine Plains.

32

The American Rhineland: Rhinebeck

DISTANCES: Loop A, 9.7 miles; Loop B, 12.4 miles

CUMULATIVE ELEVATION GAIN: Loop A, 370 feet; Loop B, 345 feet

TERRAIN: Small hills

DIFFICULTY: Easy

RECOMMENDED BICYCLE: Mountain, hybrid, road

DIRECTIONS

From the east side of the river at the Kingston-Rhinecliff Bridge, take the first right off NY 199 onto River Road (CR 103). You'll see Loop B bike route signs—don't follow them yet! Bear left onto Mt. Rutsen Road, and as you approach the village, go right onto US 9. Enter the village of Rhinebeck. At the traffic light in town (White Corner, corner of NY 308 and US 9), bear left (a sign in the intersection indicates the municipal parking lot). Go past the first municipal lot on your left to the next, much larger one on your left on East Market Street (CR 308). You'll see this large parking lot across the street from the firehouse.

Rhinebeck's (established in 1788) two marked loops represent the current state-of-the-art in greenway trail planning and recreational development—the kind any town could do if they wanted to badly enough (take Saugerties, for example). The Winnakee Land Trust and the Rhinebeck—Red Hook Greenway Committees have done a remarkable job of designating and marking these two bike loops through their respective historic districts, and they backed it up with a very good map. (By all means obtain a copy at the chamber of commerce on Montgomery

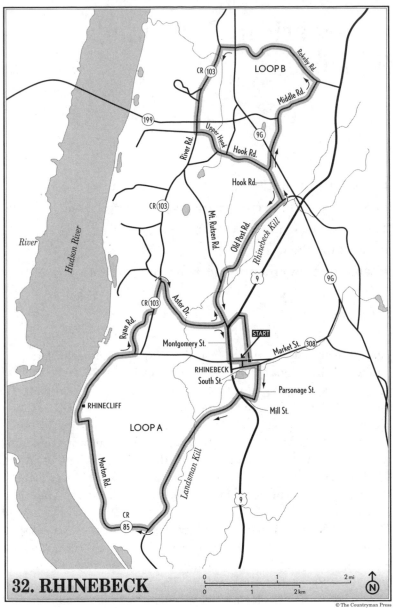

32. RHINEBECK

© The Countryman Press

Street.) I wish that every Hudson Valley town would do the same. Many are, of course. But Rhinebeck is the quintessential Hudson Valley town, a village surrounded in rich farmlands, framed by long views across the Hudson and into the Catskill Mountains.

The village itself borders hard upon the yuppified quaint, with its many interesting and original boutiques, restaurants, galleries, candy stores, antiques dealers, designer bakeries, Queen Anne–style mansions and bracketed cottages. Walking around in Rhinebeck is a worthy activity in itself. (The village also has a walking tour map.) Prices are relatively high in this bastion of the Manhattan diaspora, and you'll be hard-pressed to do a sleepover on the cheap. But you can still find ye old gnosh and swag at humane prices if you shop around. You may wish to try the awesome sliced London broil sandwich at Fosters or the eminently doable Rhinebeck Grille burger at the Rhinebeck Grille and Cantina, where Mexican is a specialty. If you want to see and be seen, by all means get a window seat at the inimitable, luscious Gigi Trattoria or any of the myriad, chichi bistros that have sprung up of late. You can also find pizza, sushi, Chinese, and a comprehensive blend of everything else from hoity-toity American regional cuisine to artsy-fartsy fusion foods. And there's always the Beekman Arms—said to be the oldest, continually open inn in North America (since 1776). After dinner, sit yourself down in the Upstate Films Theater, one of the valley's best-loved art house cinemas. There are several fine antiques shops as well.

So what about the ride? If you have time for only one loop, make it Loop A. That's where we'll begin. Note: Our mileage does not always match the handout maps, and there are some slight variations in the routes.

0.00 From the municipal parking lot on East Market Street (NY 308), follow the LOOP A bike markers. Turn left on East Market Street and follow it for two blocks, crossing Center Street.

0.10 Turn right on Mulberry Street.

0.20 Turn left on South Street and go through a quiet residential area.

Live to ride, ride to live—as long as it's got two wheels.

0.30 Right on Parsonage Street, passing Lions Park and crossing the Landsman Kill.

0.80 Turn right on Mill Street, passing the historic John Benner House (1740). Cross US 9 carefully, leaving the cemetery to your right. The road is paved and lined but lacks a shoulder. Traffic is light. The area turns semirural.

1.80 Cross the Landsman Kill by Mill Pond.

3.30 Turn right on Morton Road (CR 85). Be aware that additional, very attractive miles can be added to the south from here, off route.

3.60 The historic, 1800s mansion of Wilderstein (pronounced *will-der-styne*) appears on the left.

You may ride through the grounds to the house and have a look. It's open to the public. This was the home of Thomas Holy Suckley, a descendant of the Livingstons and a prominent local landowner. Three generations later, it belonged to Margaret Lynch Suckley, who lived there until her death in 1991 (she was born at Wilderstein in 1881). A close companion and secretary (and distant cousin) of Franklin D. Roosevelt (FDR) from the war years to his death, she is credited with giving him Fala, the infamous Scottie who became FDR's trademark pet. Because of his infidelities with Daisy, Eleanor Roosevelt separated from FDR and moved to Val-Kill.

5.50 This part is tricky, but it's easy to see the whole picture when you're there. At a triangle go left on Butler Street for two blocks, right on Grinell Street for four blocks, and right on Schatzell Street. Then turn left on Charles Street.

5.80 Rhinecliff's AMTRAK station appears here.

By all means, take a few minutes to cross the bridge and go down to the town landing next to the river. Here are excellent views of the river and the Catskill Mountains to the west. That's the Rondout lighthouse across the river, where the Rondout Creek joins the Hudson in Kingston.

Continue heading north now, as Charles Street becomes Rhinecliff Road (a.k.a. Annandale Road, CR 103).

6.50 Pass the historic Long Dock Road on the left, where a ferry operated circa 1752.

6.80 Go left on Ryan Road, which is lined with locust trees, and pass the old Creed Ankony Farm.

7.50 Turn left on River Road (a.k.a. Annandale Road, CR 103). This is a very pretty road. It carries faster traffic, but there is a shoulder of sorts. You'll ride past several beautiful estates, each with its own hand-laid stone walls.

8.00 Turn right on Astor Drive.

9.20 Turn right on Montgomery Street. (Note: If you're going to ride Loop B, do it now by turning left here and following signs, referencing mile 0.7 of Loop B.) Ride to the US 9 intersection. You can take the main drag (US 9) to the right for a more direct and more interesting route back into town. To avoid US 9, turn left and reference Loop B to return on the back roads.

9.70 Arrive at the parking lot.

LOOP B

0.00 Come out of the parking lot and turn right onto East Market Street. Be careful at the intersection.

0.10 Turn right at the light in the middle of the village onto Montgomery Street (US 9). Go along the sidewalk or carefully along the road (a signed, shared roadway), crossing Livingston and Chestnut Streets, and out onto the shoulder past Platt Avenue.

0.60 Turn left on Montgomery Street as it leaves US 9.

0.70 Leave Astor Drive to your left (Loop A).

1.20 Turn right onto Old Post Road. This is a laid-back country road.

2.70 Go left onto Hook Road.

3.10 Go right onto Middle Road (you can go either way on the loop at this point).

3.40 Cross NY 9G. Be careful—traffic is fast and furious.

3.70 Pass the Pitcher Farm, famous for its anemones. The road is paved and un-lined. The setting is rural.

4.70 Turn left onto Rokeby Road.

5.30 Bear left, continuing on Rokeby Road at the site of open fields and a large farm.

6.20 Cross NY 9G carefully, and continue on the other side, on Rokeby Road.

6.40 At a triangle, go left on River Road (CR 103). Pass Rokeby (1875).

6.70 This is the entrance to Poet's Walk Romantic Landscape Park.
If you have the energy, walk your bike through the grounds (cyclists are asked not to ride here). The trail begins with two cedar kiosks. (There's also a rustic bike rack at the trailhead, but don't leave your valuables here.) It's a very worthwhile 0.5-mile walk to the scenic, rustic gazebo that is the centerpiece of this Scenic Hudson property. Return to River Road.

Turn right on River Road. The shoulder is poor. Traffic is light but tends to be fast-moving. Pass a farm orchard and stand.

7.40 Cross NY 199 carefully, remaining on River Road. The shoulder improves only slightly.

7.50 Turn left onto Upper Hook Road.

8.00 Turn left at Hook Road and Lower Hook Road. Continue past the loop connection onto Middle Road that you took earlier.

9.20 Turn right onto Old Post Road.

10.70 Bear left, joining Montgomery Street where Old Post and Mount Rutsen Roads meet.

11.30 Cross Springbrook Avenue (US 9) carefully and bear left on the large shoulder. Now you're following Loop A back to the parking area.

11.50 Turn right on Mulberry Street, bear right again, and ride past the fairgrounds.
The Dutchess County Fair, held in late August, is the second largest agricultural event in the state.

12.20 Turn right on East Market.

12.40 You're back at the parking lot.

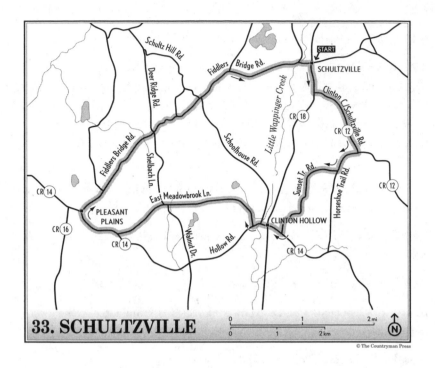

33. SCHULTZVILLE

© The Countryman Press

Hollow Lands, Hilly Lands: Schultzville

DISTANCE: 10.8 miles

CUMULATIVE ELEVATION GAIN: 800 feet

TERRAIN: Hilly

DIFFICULTY: Moderate

RECOMMENDED BICYCLE: Mountain, hybrid, road (some dirt sections)

DIRECTIONS

From the intersection of NY 199 and NY 9G (1.5 miles east of the Kingston-Rhinecliff Bridge), set to zero and go south 4.75 miles on NY 9G to CR 19 (Slate Quarry Road). Turn left (east), and at 8.5 miles, turn right (south) on CR 18 (Centre Road). At 10.7 miles, park at the intersection of CR 18 and Fiddler's Bridge Road, across the street from the General Store and Café in Schultzville, where there's an informal turnout on the side of the road.

This tour is an enticing introduction to the seemingly endless system of quiet back roads connecting the Hudson River town of Hyde Park and the dozens of little farm villages and hamlets stretching from Clinton Township to Stanford. It is here that you will dream of a world without time, where you would be free to explore every little creek and crooked path, to gaze upon each open field of wildflowers until time and times are done. We've often thought that the best way to examine the possibilities would be with an inn-to-inn approach, beginning from any-where, embarking with no special route, and ending back at the beginning. The when and where are all part of the dream.

0.00 Head out on CR 18 (Centre Road) going south.

0.35 Turn left onto Schultzville Road. This is a one-lane, dirt/paved road with a speed limit of 20 mph. Pass Apple Brook Farm (local produce) and continue through a heavily wooded area.

1.56 Turn right onto Sunset Trail, also a one-lane road with a speed limit of 20 mph.

2.00 Continue straight ahead (bearing right) on Sunset Trail, leaving Horseshoe Trail to your left. Horseshoe Trail is a prettier road than Sunset but will cost you extra mileage on CR 14 (Hollow Road) should you chose to take it.

2.30 Pass Breezy Hill Road. The road is paved now.

3.40 At CR 14, turn right and descend.

3.5 At CR 18 (Clinton Hollow Road, Centre Road) in Clinton Hollow, go straight across the intersection, carefully, onto CR 14 (Hollow Road). Cross the Little Wappinger Creek.

3.60 Schoolhouse Road appears on the right. Continue on CR 14 going west and climb easily.

3.85 Turn right onto East Meadowbrook Lane. It's a dirt road and looks like a dead end.

5.30 At a Y, continue straight ahead onto East Meadowbrook Lane (Walnut Drive goes left here). Pass Shelbach Lane (a.k.a. Sealback Lane or Seelback Road) on your right.

6.17 At a stop sign, turn right onto Hollow Road (CR 14) and go downhill a short distance. There's a loose shoulder. At the corner of Fiddler's Bridge Road in Pleasant Plains, turn right (north), passing Pleasant Plains Presbyterian Church. This is an area of gently rolling topography with a few short, steep climbs. There are Norway spruce and open fields, old farms, and sparse views across the valley to the west.

8.20 Pass Deer Ridge Road on your left.

9.00 Pass Schultz Hill Road on the left, and soon thereafter, Schoolhouse Road on the right.

Local legend has it that a bridge near here is haunted. It seems that one Halloween night in early 1900, a lone fiddler was drowned beneath the bridge in what seems were unusual circumstances. It is said that if you listen very carefully on a still Halloween Eve, you may hear faint fiddling coming from somewhere beneath the bridge.

10.60 Cross the Little Wappinger Creek.

10.80 Arrive at the general store in Schultzville.

A cyclist heads for Fiddlers Bridge to test the legend of the fiddler's ghost.

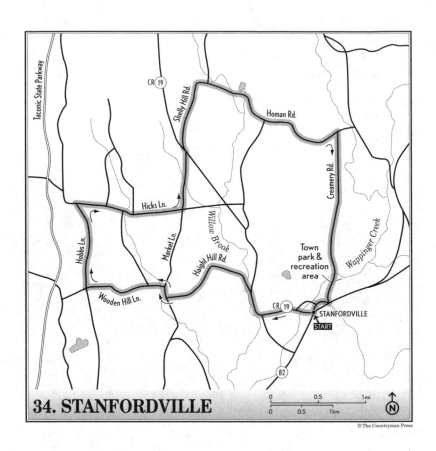

34. STANFORDVILLE

Taconic State Parkway

CR 19

Shelly Hill Rd.

Homan Rd.

Hicks Ln.

Creamery Rd.

Hobbs Ln.

Market Ln.

Willow Brook

Wappinger Creek

Haight Hill Rd.

Town park & recreation area

Wooden Hill Ln.

CR 19

STANFORDVILLE
START

82

0   0.5   1mi
0   0.5   1km

N

© The Countryman Press

Milking It: Stanfordville

DISTANCE: 10.2 miles

CUMULATIVE ELEVATION GAIN: 625 feet

TERRAIN: Mildly hilly

DIFFICULTY: Moderate

RECOMMENDED BICYCLE: Mountain, hybrid, road (some dirt sections)

DIRECTIONS

From US 44 and NY 82 off the Taconic State Parkway in Pleasant Valley (as if you were going to Millbrook), take NY 82 for 7.5 miles north to Stanfordville. Park in Market Square at the corner of CR 19 and CR 85 or proceed to the town park on Creamery Road (specific details follow).

East of the Hudson between the river towns of Tivoli and Fishkill, in an area reaching to the Connecticut state line, is a world of wooded hollows and fecund farms. Many of the early villages, settled long ago by farmers from Massachusetts and Connecticut who were seeking the open space to the west, retain a New England–like colonial charm. Large tracts of land, much of it owned by a few or several individuals (such as the Nine Partners Patent), remained intact long enough to preserve a good deal of the wild character you see today. Stanfordville is such a town—a place that has, either by coincidence or design, retained its agrarian character from its beginnings, around 1750 (incorporated in 1793). Today, the major industry is dairy farming.

As you arrive in Stanfordville, which is not much more than an intersection between two other intersections (Bangall to the north and Clinton Corners to the south), the first thing you will see is Market Square. There's a general store and a bakery here. You could in fact leave your car here after enjoying a short break from your drive and a rich treat from the bakery, but there's a better spot around the corner. Go behind Market Square on Church Road and then up Creamery Road to the north, passing the Stanford Free Library on your right. There's a small town park, recreation area, and good-sized parking area on the right about 0.4 mile from Market Square. From there, return to CR 19 (Bulls Head Road) at Market Square to begin the tour.

0.00 Take CR 19 (Bulls Head Road), heading west. Cross the Wappinger Creek. There's a double line here, still within the village limits, but the traffic is light. There is a fog line and a bit of a shoulder. Watch to the left for Haight Hill Road.

0.82 At Haight Hill Road, go left. Cross the bridge over Willow Brook. Climb Haight Hill, where you'll be treated to northerly views of Stissing Mountain in Pine Plains. Descend to the corner of Haight Hill Road and Market Lane.

2.00 Turn right onto Market Lane.

2.10 Go left onto Prospect Hill Road (a.k.a. Wooden Hill Road).

3.00 Turn right onto Willow Brook Road (a.k.a. Hobbs Lane) and travel north.

3.90 Turn right onto Hicks Lane. At the beginning of a steep hill, there's a double line. Climb.

5.10 Turn left at the corner of Market and Hicks Lanes and go north toward CR 19. Locust trees and maple thickets adorn the roadsides.

5.60 Cross CR 19 directly onto Shelly Hill Road and climb.

6.60 At the intersection of Homan and Shelly Hill Roads, bear right onto Homan Road. This is a one-lane road with no lines. This section is more secluded.

7.27 At the intersection of Homan and Bowan Roads, bear left, remaining on Homan Road.

Today, the major industry in Schultzville is dairy farming.

8.20 At a stop sign at Creamery and Homan Roads (next to the elementary school), go right onto Creamery Road. Travel south, toward Stanfordville. Cross the Wappinger Creek.

9.70 As you ascend after crossing the Wappinger Creek, immediately on your left is the town park and recreation area.

10.20 Arrive at Market Square.

Val-Kill cottage, the Eleanor Roosevelt Historic Site

35

I Was a Shy, Solemn Child: Val-Kill

DISTANCE: 4 miles

CUMULATIVE ELEVATION GAIN: 100 feet

TERRAIN: Slightly hilly

DIFFICULTY: Easy

RECOMMENDED BICYCLE: Mountain

DIRECTIONS

Park at the FDR National Historic Site in Hyde Park, 6 miles north of Poughkeepsie on US 9 (Albany Post Road). Parking is free, and you can enter the visitor center for information and orientation.

About the only value the story of my life may have, is to show that one can, even without any particular gifts, overcome obstacles that seem insurmountable if one is willing to face the fact that they must be overcome. —Eleanor Roosevelt

This is a very interesting, short tour that connects Springwood, the birthplace and home of Franklin D. Roosevelt, with Val-Kill, the home of his estranged wife, Anna Eleanor Roosevelt. The two separated when Eleanor discovered FDR's infidelities with his secretary, Daisy. It was decided that they would remain married, but Eleanor would take up residence in a cottage that was built for her on the Val-Kill Creek, a place west of Springwood where the two had been fond of picnicking. Although separated physically from FDR, Eleanor remained the faithful eyes and ears of the president, who in spite of her shy nature, grew up to conduct an active political life of her own, defining a new role for the first lady as she took an active part in world affairs.

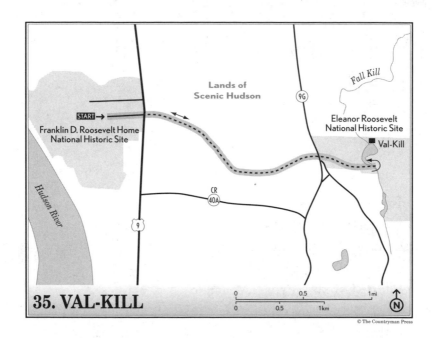

35. VAL-KILL

© The Countryman Press

Your visit to Val-Kill begins at the FDR home, library, and museum, which are both operated by the National Park Service. You are also in the vicinity of the Vanderbilt Mansion and only a mile or so from the Culinary Institute of America, the former Jesuit seminary where the visionary priest Tielhard de Chardin lived, taught, and is buried. (Many say Chardin predicted the Internet). With some planning, you can visit all four of these Hudson Valley gems (at least take the time to drive through the Vanderbilt grounds for one of the best views of the Catskills), finishing with a repast at the CIA's Apple Pie Café and Bakery.

Bicyclists should be aware that there is a foot trail system at the FDR National Historic Site (Roosevelt Woods) that is off limits to bicycles, as is the dirt loop trail at Val-Kill, lying southwest of the cottage.

From the (free) parking area at the FDR home, library, and museum, walk your bike south to a point between the Henry A. Wallace Visitor Center and the library/museum complex. Look to your left on the trees for the HYDE PARK TRAIL markers, a green tulip poplar leaf on a white background. Follow the markers across US 9 where the Hyde Park Trail enters the woods at a map and information kiosk just north of the Hyde Park Brewing Company parking lot. (There is also room to park at this trailhead.)

0.00 Head into the woods on a dirt road. This is a stable surface for the most part, but it has become badly eroded in places due to heavy, unregulated ATV abuse. This large parcel belongs to Scenic Hudson, a tract that was purchased with the help of the Winnake Land Trust and the Hudson Valley Greenway. There may be some small but muddy stream crossings.

1.50 Cross NY 9G into the Val-Kill National Historic Site and follow the paved road to the cottage complex.

2.00 In the driveway alongside the house, there's a bicycle rack. You can lock your bike up here and take a look around.

Franklin and Eleanor were kissing cousins; they began to date when Eleanor was doing social work in New York City. They were joined in marriage by then President Theodore Roosevelt (Uncle Ted). She was active in the New Deal program and was asked by President Truman to chair the United Nations Human Rights Commission. She led the drafting of the Declaration of Human Rights, which Mrs. Roosevelt considered the single most important accomplishment of her life.

Eleanor was much happier living at Val-Kill. It was here that she could do her work uninterrupted and where she could invite friends without the permission of her domineering mother-in-law. It was here that she hosted dignitaries—Churchill, Khrushchev, JFK, and Nehru among them. Val-Kill Cottage, the Depression-era workshop where Eleanor conducted various training programs for local farmers (and also where she lived), is open to visitors. So is the Stone Cottage, the site's first residence.

Eleanor contracted a bone marrow disease and died on November 7, 1962. She had previously given Springwood to the federal government, but Val-Kill was sold to a private developer. Encouraged by a local citizens' group, President Jimmy Carter signed legislation creating the Eleanor Roosevelt National Historic Site in May 1977.

When you're finished looking through the cottage and grounds, return the way you came. If you've got the time, the site's Meadow Trail makes a wonderful short walk. Also visit Roosevelt's gravesite and take a look at Springwood, FDR's birthplace. (There's a fee to enter the house, library, and museum, but not for the visitor center.) For information, contact Superintendent, Roosevelt-Vanderbilt National Historic Sites, 519 Albany Post Road, Hyde Park, NY 12538-1997. The telephone is 845-229-9115 and the web site is www.nps.gov/elro.

Oil and Ecosystems: Millbrook and the Mary Flagler Cary Arboretum

DISTANCE: 8.45 miles

CUMULATIVE ELEVATION GAIN: 275 feet

TERRAIN: Hilly

DIFFICULTY: Moderate

RECOMMENDED BICYCLE: Mountain, hybrid, road (some dirt sections)

DIRECTIONS

The Institute of Ecosystem Studies (IES) at the Mary Flagler Cary Arboretum in Millbrook is on NY 44A, approached on US 44 from the west or from the east and northeast. You can reach US 44 from the Taconic State Parkway. Parking for the tour is in the village of Millbrook on US 44. Come into the village on US 44 and park at Tribute Gardens parking lot in Millbrook proper, which you'll see at the corner of North Avenue and Franklin Street. Before the tour you should get your (free) visitor pass and map at the Gifford House Visitor and Education Center on NY 44A, where you may also park—but the lot may be full on busy weekends.

Perhaps no other village in Dutchess County is as synonymous with money and horse farms as Millbrook. Suffice it to say that the place oozes opulence. But Millbrook's is *old* money, and Mary Flagler Cary's was oil money. Even better, it's quiet money. Everything is in good taste. And unless you get back into the countryside to ogle covetously at the town's breeding and dressage farms and its plethoric, hunt country mansions, you'd think Millbrook was just a prettier-than-usual Hudson Valley village (and it is).

Those of us who are unimpressed by the cornucopia of worldly possessions (it will be easier for you if you think of the vet bills and the taxes) will find more to like in Millbrook's natural wealth. Its inventory includes open spaces, scenic viewsheds, rich woodlands, and quiet, eminently bikable back roads. It is a place where the roads are clean, the homes are lovely, and the open space is managed wisely.

After you park or before you leave, by all means take a short walk up Franklin Street, where there are some quaint little shops and eateries, an old-fashioned diner, and a Stewarts shop, which is making an awkward attempt to fit in as a storefront. But if you really want a short tour of the area's fine homesteads, have a look at the listings in the realtors' windows.

0.00 Head north out of the parking lot onto North Avenue, which will lead you over the east branch of Wappinger Creek onto Stanford Road.

0.85 Cross NY 44A with caution, continuing on Stanford Road. This is a very nice paved and unlined country road at this point. The creek is on your left.

2.30 Turn left onto Woodstock Road (dirt), where you'll ride past ponds and horse farms.

3.70 Continue straight ahead, leaving Petit Road to your left. Note: Petit Road goes south to meet Canoe Hill Road and would, in fact, allow for a fine short loop back to Stanford Road, cutting out the worst (fastest) section of NY 44A (a.k.a. Sharon Turnpike). If you choose this option, turn left off Petit Road as you join Canoe Hill Road and turn left on NY 44A.

4.80 Turn left (south) on NY 82. There's a wide shoulder. The Mid-Hudson Bicycle Club maintains this section of the road.

5.20 Turn left (east) onto Canoe Hill Road, a paved road with no lines.

5.80 Go straight onto Fowler Road as Canoe Hill Road goes off to the left. Now, isn't this beautiful farm country?

6.00 Continue straight ahead as you leave Nardone Road to your right.

6.25 Turn right onto the IES Woodcock Drive. This is a very pleasant, mellow

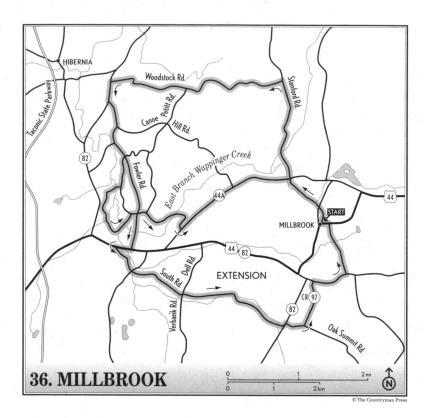

36. MILLBROOK

© The Countryman Press

road that will give you a close-up look at the IES ecological field research facility. There are no lines and what traffic there is goes very slowly.

6.50 Turn right again.

Note the tree swallows nesting here—they've taken over some of the eastern bluebird boxes you'll see along the way. Cross the east branch of Wappinger Creek.

6.70 Bear left.

If you want to see the greenhouse, bear right at this point and go 0.2 mile to carefully cross NY 82. The greenhouse is directly across the road. There's a bike rack in the visitors' parking lot.

7.90 Bear right at the intersection.

8.00 Go straight across Fowler Road (to extend this tour, see the Alternative that follows this section) onto Lovelace Drive. Climb and then descend.

8.80 Cross the creek.

Just past this point, on your right, you will see the beautiful Fern Glen, where you can take a break to have a look at herbaceous peat lands, shrub swamps, ponds, deciduous forests, and hemlock forests. Lock your bike and take a look—this path comes highly recommended.

9.20 At the point where Lovelace Drive joins IES Drive, where you can see the Plant Science Building and Gene E. Likens Laboratory to your right, bear left onto NY 44A. (Dr. Likens is the scientist who documented the existence of acid rain during his work at Hubbard Brook Forest in New Hampshire.) There's a good shoulder here, and good sight distance, but there's frequently fast-moving traffic.

9.80 Pass the Gifford House Visitor and Education Center.

11.00 Turn right onto Stanford Road and retrace the route back to North Avenue.

12.00 Arrive at the parking area in Millbrook.

ALTERNATIVE

To extend this tour with added miles through Millbrook Heights, bear right on Fowler Road at mile 8. This route is 5.7 miles with 245 feet of vertical gain.

0.00 Turn right (west) on Fowler Road.

0.50 Turn right onto US 44 and NY 82. There's a good shoulder. Traffic can be heavy, but there's a speed zone here as you approach Washington Hollow, which keeps it sane.

0.80 Carefully cross US 44 and NY 82 and turn left onto South Road. Travel east-southeast, uphill, into Millbrook Heights. This is high, open country. There's a bit of suburbia here and there, and some interesting architecture.

2.00 Pass shady Dell Road and Verbank Road intersection.

3.60 Turn left onto NY 82.

3.70 Turn right onto Oak Summit Road (lined) to avoid travel on NY 82.

3.90 Turn left on County House Road (CR 97) and climb.

4.60 Bear right at CR 111 and follow it a short distance to CR 343, at the site of Bennet College.

5.10 Go left onto Church Street (unlined, paved) at the site of Nine Partners Cemetery.

5.90 Arrive in Millbrook at the corner of Church and Franklin Streets, and turn left. You'll see the parking area just ahead, a block or so away. For general IES information, call 845-677-5359. The IES web site is www.ecostudies.org.

Putnam County

The Bird and Bottle and the Sunken Mine: Northern Putnam

DISTANCE: 21 miles

CUMULATIVE ELEVATION GAIN: 3000 feet

TERRAIN: Hilly

DIFFICULTY: Strenuous

RECOMMENDED BICYCLE: Mountain, hybrid, road (several dirt sections)

DIRECTIONS

Begin the tour from Clarence Fahnestock Memorial State Park. From US 9D in Cold Spring, follow NY 310 for 2.4 miles to US 9. Cross US 9 and follow NY 301 to the Pelton Pond parking area for a total of 7.9 miles from Cold Spring (or come west 0.6 mile from the NY 301 exit off the Taconic State Parkway). Park opposite the park headquarters building at Pelton Pond. You can shorten the tour by 6.5 miles by parking at the Dennytown Road trailhead parking area (see mile 3.4).

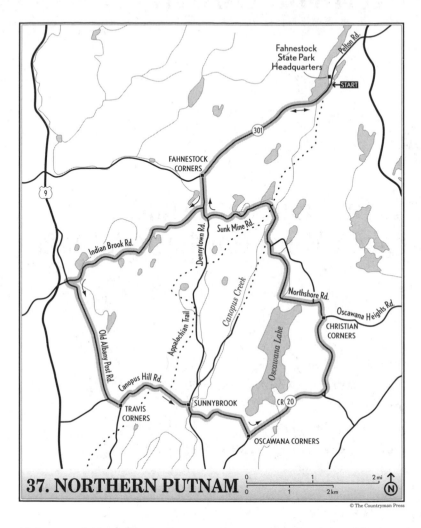

37. NORTHERN PUTNAM

© The Countryman Press

Fahnestock Park lies in the extensive woodlands of the old iron mining country of Northern Putnam County. The Taconic Region of the New York State Office of Parks, Recreation, and Historic Preservation administers its nearly 7 thousand acres. In the late 1800s, the Pennsylvania and Reading Coal and Iron Company ceased operations in this area, but many of the mines remain, making interesting destinations for the hikers of today. Some of the mines were flooded (thus, *Sunk Mine*) during the 1930s with the creation of Canopus Lake by the Civilian Conservation Corps. You won't see a mine on this trip, but you will travel the old roads that led to them—several miles of which still look as they did over 150 years ago. You'll also travel a section of the oldest state road in the Colonies, the Post Road, dating from 1669. You will also pass the historic Bird and Bottle Inn (1761), a gourmet restaurant with guest accommodations.

0.00 Leave the Pelton Pond parking area and turn left (west) onto NY 301. There is moderate traffic on this lined and paved road.

3.00 Turn left onto Dennytown Road at Fahnestock Corners.

3.40 Turn right onto Indian Brook Road (a.k.a. Stow Road, Freedie Reeves Road). If you continue 0.15 mile straight ahead on Dennytown Road, you will come to the trailhead parking area on the left, at the corner of Sunk Mine and Dennytown Roads. The surface is mostly hard dirt.

6.00 Turn left onto Old Albany Post Road. After stopping in for a good night's rest and repast, leave the gorgeous edifice of the Bird and Bottle Inn to your right and bear left at a Y, remaining on Old Albany Post Road.

The Bird and Bottle was originally known as Warren's Tavern and was an important state coach stop on the Old Post Road. The road was created as a postal route to Albany at a time when Benjamin Franklin was postmaster general. It followed a Native American route called The Path. The road was widened to carry supplies for the French and Indian War effort. Later it was used by Washington's troops and formed an important connection between the iron mines and the West Point Foundry in Garrison (Continental Village). Franklin had milestones placed from Manhattan to Albany to determine the cost of shipping. It is said that this 6-mile section of the road retains much of its early character.

8.00 Arrive at Travis Corners. Bear left.

8.15 Turn left onto Canopus Hill Road and descend. There are no shoulders.

9.14 The Appalachian Trail (AT) comes in from the south at this point, crossing Conopus Hill Road.

9.50 At Canopus Hollow Road, turn right.

9.60 Turn left onto Sunset Hill Road and climb steeply through Sunnybrook.

10.76 Turn left onto CR 20, at Oscawana Corners. There's a deli on the left. A few dull miles of paved and fairly busy roads follow (the price that must be paid to reach the Sunk Mine Road).

13.45 Turn left onto Northshore Road at Christian Corners. Oscawana Heights Road goes off to the right (east). Northshore Road takes you around the north end of Oscawana Lake.

14.35 Turn right onto unpaved, unmaintained Sunk Mine Road. A paved road continues straight ahead at this point but soon dead-ends. It does not cross Candlewood Hill. Now you are back in Fahnestock Park and will enjoy a remote and scenic climb through the astonishing and deeply forested Canopus Creek ravine. You'll ride amid dense hemlock forests, passing several isolated ponds and hiking trailheads. The ravine falls away steeply to the left.

16.10 Cross the AT again.

17.20 Arrive at Dennytown Road, next to the trailhead parking area, and turn right.

18.00 Turn right onto NY 301.

21.00 Arrive at the Pelton Pond parking lot.

Band of Gypsies: Carmel

DISTANCE: 14.7 miles

CUMULATIVE ELEVATION GAIN: 865 feet

TERRAIN: Hilly

DIFFICULTY: Moderate

RECOMMENDED BICYCLE: Mountain, hybrid, road

DIRECTIONS

Carmel is 6 miles west of Brewster on US 6. The tour begins just north of US 6, at the intersection of CR 47 and CR 52, at the northeast corner of Lake Gleneida, the main intersection in the village of Carmel. (County routes 301 and 47 also intersect here). Parking can be a problem on this busy thoroughfare, although there is plenty of parking (time limit) adjacent to Veteran's Memorial Park next to the lake. It is possible to park at the rail trail parking area on US 6, 0.5 mile south of the intersection, coming to the starting point by following US 6 or detouring onto the more sedate Seminary Road and Church Street.

The extensive reservoir system in the town of Carmel is a cyclist's mecca. This area includes the East Branch Croton Diverting Reservoir, the Croton Falls and Middle Branch Reservoir, Lake Mayopac, and the West Branch and Boyd Corners reservoirs. Because of the connecting state and county roads and a latticework of lightly traveled town roads, the potential for interesting cycle routes in this area is unlimited. Because these roads are so popular with cyclists, most of them have been designated as shared roadways, so motorists have become attuned to the presence of cyclists on the reservoirs' scenic road system.

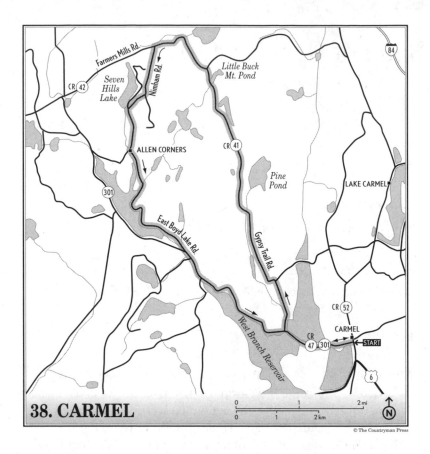

38. CARMEL

© The Countryman Press

However, this does not mean a cyclist can let their guard down. Because of the scenic nature of this appealing road system, motorists tend to be distracted and this fact requires a defensive riding style. In addition, most of the riders who use the area are experienced touring enthusiasts, many of whom practice a very high level of training and fitness and have a high degree of familiarly with the area's systems and traffic patterns. Correspondingly, motorists have come to expect a certain degree of protocol from cyclists, anticipating that they will keep to the fog line or shoulder and will deliberately signal their intentions at turns and intersections. It is gratifying to see such a cooperative relationship between the cycling and driving public, and the roads of northern Putnam County seem to be the only ones in the Hudson Valley where this relationship is so apparent.

This hilly loop ride will introduce you to local, state, and county highways, as well as the backroad routes connecting them, providing just a small sample of the varied and interesting riding experience that visitors to Putnam can enjoy, and that local residents rejoice in.

0.00 From the CR 47 intersection in Carmel, go west on West Street (CR 47 and NY 301). Soon you will have views of the West Branch Reservoir. The shoulders are not useful, but the traffic is bike-friendly.

Cross the causeway separating the north and south basins of the West Branch Reservoir. Turn right onto Gypsy Trail Road (CR 41). Now you will leave the reservoir and climb into Ninham Mountain State Forest). Pass Veteran's Memorial Park. Head downhill. Pass the Ninham Mountain State Forest headquarters and, slightly beyond that, the forest ranger residence. This state forest and multi-use area is popular with mountain bikers.

4.00 North of the state forest, you will come to the Gypsy Trail Club.

Here you'll find a large, rustic log clubhouse, surrounded by a small community of seasonal cottages. At first this area may seem to appear to you as a private dead end; and though the club, in fact, is private, Gypsy Trail Road continues through the community, to the north. Be advised that Maynard Road, which is shown on most recent maps as heading northwest to Upper Lake Ninham, is private. After admiring the elegant lodge clubhouse, continue north on Gypsy Trail Road as the road undulates through beautiful woods.

5.60 Pass Little Buck Mountain Pond on the right.

5.80 Arrive at Farmers Mills Road (CR 42). Turn left. The speed limit is 35 mph and the road is lined.

7.10 Pass the historic society cottage on your left and turn left. Bear left immediately thereafter onto Ninham Road. Turn left and ascend. Watch the blind curves as the road flattens out.

7.90 Bear right at Lacrosse Road and descend. The speed limit is 30 mph. Descend through Allen Corners.

9.00 Bear left onto East Boyd Lake Road (a.k.a. Boyd's Corners Road). Traveling through a pretty wooded area, you will have glimpses of Boyd Corners Reservoir on your right.

11.20 At CR 47 and NY 301, bear left onto West Carmel–Kent Cliffs Road. The wide shoulder soon shrinks, so command your space here and drive defensively. Now you are riding along the northwest arm of the West Branch Reservoir. The traffic is considerate, but often the pretty scenery absorbs the drivers, so stay hard to the right.

13.50 Having completed the loop to Gypsy Trail Road again, bear right and cross the causeway.

14.70 Arrive at the intersection where you began.

Appendix: Bike Shop Listings

THE CATSKILLS (TOURS 1-14)

Overlook Mountain Bikes
93 Tinker St.
Woodstock, NY 12498
845-679-2122

Philthy O's
6000 Main St.
Tannersville, NY 12485
518-589-0600

Kingston Cyclery
1094 Morton Blvd.
Kingston, NY 12401
845-382-2453

Big Wheel
1774 Ulster Ave.
Lake Katrine, NY 12449
845-382-2444

Table Rock Tours and Bicycles
292 Main St.
Rosendale, NY 12472
845-658-7832

Windham Mountain Outfitters
2 County Road 12
South Windham, NY 04062
518-734-4700

THE SHAWANGUNKS (TOURS 15-19)

Accord Bicycle Service
Route 209
Kerhonkson, NY 12446
845-626-7214

The Bicycle Depot
15 Main St.
New Paltz, NY 12561
845-255-3859

The Bicycle Rack
13 North Front St.
New Paltz, NY 12561
845-255-1770

Table Rock Tours and Bicycles
292 Main St.
Rosendale, NY 12472
845-658-7832

COLUMBIA COUNTY (TOURS 20-27)

Bash Bish Bicycles
247 Route 344
West Copake, NY 12516
518-329-4962

Charlies' Bike Shop
Route 22
North Hillsdale, NY 12529
518-325-3986

DUTCHESS COUNTY (TOURS 28-36)

Rhinebeck Bicycle Shop
10 Garden St.
Rhinebeck, NY 12572
845-876-4025

Village Bicycles
57 S. Center St.
Millerton, NY 12546
518-789-7813

Performance Pedal
Route 9
Hyde Park, NY 12538
845-229-5138

The Bicycle Shop
Route 44
Pleasant Valley, NY 12569
845-635-3161

PUTNAM COUNTY (TOURS 37-38)

Bikeway Bicycles
692 Route 6
Mahopac, NY 10541
845-621-2800
www.bikeway.com

Bikeway Bicycles
1581 Route 376 (Corner of New
Hackensack Rd.)
Wappingers Falls, NY 12590
845-621-2800
www.bikeway.com

Village Bicycle Shop
97 Old Route 6
Carmel, NY 10512
845-225-5982